71-63

MY BROTHER
IS A STRANGER

MY BROTHER IS A STRANGER

COMPILED BY
BRUCE HILTON

Friendship Press · New York

TABLE OF CONTENTS

Supplementary items following "Instant City" and
"More of Everything" are by the Editor

INTRODUCTION

Not long ago i stood with a German friend in Berlin and looked over the wall at a group of East Zone teen-agers playing soccer in a field.

"My brother is over there somewhere," my friend said. "But I do not expect to see him again.

"I suppose," he went on, "that if we did meet, he would seem like a stranger after so long a time."

Since that day I have been aware of many other walls dividing brother from brother. They are here in our own cities.

When people are crowded together in the city, life is much different from what it was back in the country. You know many more people, but you don't know any of them well. And custom, prejudice, or the cost of housing cuts the city up into little walled sections. Certain Negroes live here, and Negroes of another class live there; $15,000 suburbanites live here and $25,000 suburbanites live there; Southern mountaineers live here and immigrants live there.

But the city is getting shaken up. Growing too fast for its own good, the city is changing daily because of slum clearance, redevelopment, automation, blockbusting, and mobility.

In this book you'll meet some of the people caught in this shake-up—people who are your brothers in Christ, whether you and your church recognize them as brothers or not.

Bruce Hilton

EXCEPT FOR THE FEW MOMENTS when we were going down that dark alley after the man with the gun, it was pretty quiet for a Saturday night.

Sergeant Morris had warned that it might be. Earlier in the evening, as we had climbed into the dark blue police cruiser for a night tour of the city, he had asked, "So you want to see the city the way a police officer sees it. Why?"

"Well," I tried to explain, "as a church worker I ought

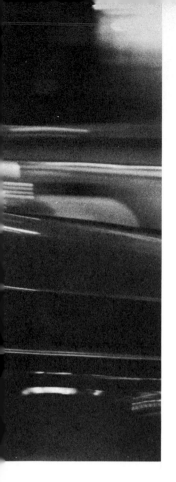

SQUAD CAR

to know more about it. Most of us never really see the city. I spent the day at Daily Vacation Bible School with junior high youth who have no idea what other parts of the city are like.

"But you policemen see the city as it really is."

He smiled. "It might be a slow night. But I'll try to show you a different view of the city." He eased the cruiser out of the headquarters parking lot and into the traffic.

"We'll start right close here, at the edge of the slum clearance area. Got a call about a boy making trouble."

We turned a corner and suddenly there weren't any buildings to the east. An area five or six blocks wide and a half-mile long had been cleared—every building flattened, every brick and board carted away.

Like islands among the weeds, two little brick churches stood, far apart, in the gloom.

"Once this was 'Germantown,'" the sergeant said. "One of the nicest parts of town, but half the people didn't speak English at all, and the rest liked you better if you spoke German. They built those two churches. But that was years ago. They moved out, the big houses got divided up for tenements, and it got pretty bad over here. The federal government helped clear this; now they'll find somebody to build apartment buildings."

"But where did the people go who lived here?"

"To other slums—nearly all of them. Some of them moved in with relatives. And they were probably already crowded into half enough space.

"Most of these folks were from the hill country down south, where families stick together. Their kinfolk up here would find them a place."

We were pulling up in front of a house on Apple Street, where a fat man was signaling to us. He stuck his head in the car window.

"That's the boy across the street, sitting on the porch," the man whispered. "He's always making trouble; he picked up this little four-year-old boy and slammed him down on the sidewalk; the kid's got bruises all over."

He straightened up and beckoned toward another house,

where a young woman sat on the rickety front porch. We noticed little groups of people sitting on the steps or lounging under trees all up and down the street. The houses were packed tightly together and the paint was dirty and peeling.

The young woman came over, holding a little boy by the hand, and at Sergeant Morris's invitation they got into the back seat of the cruiser.

"This is the boy who got hurt," the fat man said. "See those bruises and scrapes?"

The youngster looked at the policeman, wide-eyed but silent.

"That older kid is always in trouble," the man went on. "We even thought about getting up a petition, asking his family to move. Can't you do something about it?"

"This is a case for the juvenile squad," Morris said. "I'll give 'thirty-seven' a radio call and they'll be out here, in plain clothes, just as soon as they can."

A few minutes later, as we drove away, most of the people hadn't even moved off their porches to see why we were there. "What will happen to the boy?" I asked.

"Well, car thirty-seven will contact the child's mother, and get her to sign an assault and battery complaint. Then they'll talk to the parents of the teen-ager—to see if he really is vicious or if he just did this playing around and didn't know any better.

"He may just get a stiff lecture, or he might end up in the detention home."

He laughed. "Did you notice how hardly anybody paid attention to us? They're used to having the police settle their neighborhood arguments.

ALARM!

DANGER!

"Now in Hamilton Heights," he grinned, "most people would have a stroke if a police cruiser parked in front of their house for five minutes!"

We were cruising back through the bare slum clearance area. "The people who were here wouldn't call the police either. They'd settle it themselves, the way they would back home—a little cuttin' with a switchblade, or a little shootin'. Doesn't mean much to them—and they sure get mad when the police arrive to break it up!"

Suddenly, as though a boundary line had been passed, everybody on the streets was Negro. We were on the west side, where 80 per cent of the city's Negroes live because they can't buy a house anywhere else.

It was a balmy night, and every home, every store, and every bar had a little knot of people in front. Some had brought out chairs, and were tilted back against the building, relaxed, watching.

"The folks around here sure look forward to Saturday night," Sergeant Morris said.

"Look at 'em; they ain't hurtin' anybody—just looking."

As we rolled slowly down the streets, somebody would

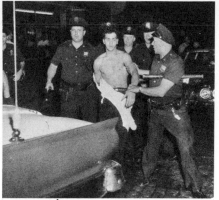

CAPTURE!

occasionally recognize the cruiser's passing with a shouted wisecrack or a wave of derision.

"But we've had our nights here, too," he went on. "Just a month ago, on a real hot night, we had a riot here—they were throwing bricks down on the cruisers from buildings, and this street was packed solid with yelling people. . . ."

He stopped short. "That's a gambling joint," he said, nodding toward a little store front with dirty windows and a faded sign, "Charlie's Shine Parlor."

"Let's go in and bust it up. They're shooting craps in the back."

We parked the cruiser up the block and started walking back toward the shine parlor.

"That guy in the front window, behind the venetian blind. He's the 'buzzer,'" the sergeant said. "He's signaling them in the back room right now."

The man waved through the window at us as we turned into the place. "Hi, Sergeant. How are ya?"

"Just fine, just fine. Anything on in the back room?"

Just then the door to the back room burst open and the short, tubby proprietor came hustling out.

13

"Hi, there, Sergeant, how are ya?" He was all smiles. "What's new?"

"Hi. Just thought we'd have a look at your back room."

"Why, sure, come on back!" Tubby led the way through three heavy doors—two opening out and one opening in—into a large, barren room. In the center was a big round green table, covered with felt. The two men who sat at the table nodded to us.

The back doors were boarded up, I noticed. Sergeant Morris exchanged a few more meaningless words with the proprietor, and we turned to go out.

"You have to have the money and the dice as evidence to get a gambling conviction," he explained as we made our way back through the three sets of doors. "They were gone—probably down a chute—before we walked in the front door. But we slowed things down for a while.

"We've tried tricks, and we've tried rushing the place, but the only time we've ever caught this guy with the goods was on Halloween. A vice squad member in a costume wandered in, and was in the back room before they knew who he was!

"People wonder why we keep hammering at these little games. They call them little.

"Well, a guy came up to me while I was sitting in the car right along this street last week; he had tears running down his face. He had lost his whole pay check.

"Some fast talker had convinced him he could beat the house in one of these little gambling joints—and of course the guy who talked him into it was really a shill for the man running the game. That family had a rough time that week, and the man had kids too. If this stuff only affected

BUT THERE'S EXCITEMENT OF ANOTHER KIND IN A POLICEMAN'S LIFE. THERE'S THE ADVENTURE OF BEING A FRIEND, A HELPER, A PART OF THE COMMUNITY.

the gambler, then O.K. But this guy had slaved all week for that money, and now his family goes hungry.

"When something like this affects the family it affects the whole community. And that's why we keep going after these 'little' games."

Soon we were back in the car, heading over the river that splits the city in two.

"It's funny," Sam said. "These colored people east of the river don't associate much with the people on the west side. They're less trouble, too. You just can't lump 'em all together because they're the same color."

For an hour we just cruised slowly around the city. We passed rows of bars on East Fifth Street, where tall, lean young men just up from the hills of Kentucky and Tennessee met people from back home.

We drove down a quiet street in Homewood, a neighborhood that has become predominantly Negro in the last five years. "Increase in crime rate? No," the Sergeant said, "you can check, but as far as I know, the change from white to colored hasn't brought any more crime to Homewood."

We cruised along the fringes of a "better" neighborhood on the north side. "Some of these folks would have a fit if their neighbors saw a cruiser parked in front of their house," he said with a grin. "But these suburban people have their problems too—kids whose mothers are working or gone all day to clubs.

"These kids cause real havoc, but their dads pay for the damage and keep people from calling the police."

Closer to the heart of town, we passed a tiny store front church, with "Church of the Holy Spirit Deliverance" scrawled in poster paint on the window. The sounds of sing-

16

ing and clapping rose and then faded away as we rolled past.

In the next block stood a huge, red brick church. "Soon to reopen as Mt. Zion Baptist Church," said the neat sign in the front yard. Once the building had housed the largest congregation of its denomination in the city; two of its pastors had been elected bishops. Now its congregation (white) had merged with another church, and a Negro congregation had bought the building.

The police radio had been amazingly silent for Saturday night, but suddenly it crackled again. "Go to 808 Epley Street. Report a man with a stolen gun."

The cruiser wheeled around in a tight U turn and pulled to a stop in front of the Epley Street address just a block away.

A noisy and cheerful crowd had quickly gathered, attracted by the squad car already on the scene. It was a dark, dingy street. A row of houses were built solidly one right on to the other. We walked into the front room of the house where we had seen the two patrolmen go in.

Just as we did, a teen-age girl came running into the house from the back.

"He's out in back now," she said. "He's got the gun out in the alley."

I followed Sam and the two patrolmen out the front door and down the street which paralleled the alley behind the homes. I noticed Sam loosening the flap on his holster, as he looked for a break in the row of houses where we could cut through to the alley.

As we rounded the corner of the block one of the patrolmen looked over his shoulder. "You armed?" I shook my head. He looked at the sergeant, who nodded assurance, and I started walking faster to be a little bit closer to him.

Now we were in the dark alley and I was picking out places to duck, just in case I'd need to, when a figure loomed out of the darkness. Sam, who had taken his gun out of his holster as we turned the corner, ordered the stranger to get his hands in the air. The two patrolmen moved in and held his arms, frisking him quickly at the same time. "Just let me explain," the man kept shouting as the patrolman held him. "Just give me a chance to explain."

"Are you Arnold Brown?" Sergeant Morris asked.

"Yes, but I wanna explain; I just took the gun away from him because I didn't want him to shoot his wife. He was shootin' the gun into the ground, and she was afraid, and she asked me to take the gun away, and I took it away and I told him I would give it back to him in the morning. . . ."

With the protesting Brown walking between the two patrolmen, we started back down the unlighted alley in the direction of the first house we'd been in.

Brown had announced that the gun he was accused of stealing was at his house, about a block and a half away. We'd have to go get it.

Eventually, Brown was taken to jail along with the gun owner, who had admitted shooting it into the ground five times. But it is not the sight of the men in the back of the squad car, or the sight of the gun-owner's wife cheerfully demanding twenty dollars with which to come down and bail him out in the morning, that sticks in my mind.

It is what I saw at Arnold Brown's house when we went to get the gun. We came by the back door into a crowded kitchen. We could see a tiny bathroom, without a door, and a little bedroom that was barely large enough for a double bed.

"It's under the mattress," Brown said. The sergeant lifted the thin, lumpy mattress and found the gun—a miniature .22 revolver—under the second corner he tried.

I turned back to the kitchen—and looked straight into the wide eyes of an eight-year-old curly-headed boy. Behind him stood his brother, about a year younger. I tried a weak smile, but the older youngster just looked away from me into the face of his father. "Never mind, Eli," the father said.

Eli looked at the gun, and at the policeman who had a firm hold on his father's elbow, then he turned away with his brother and walked to the other side of the kitchen table.

I remember the police and Brown walking out the door. I know they met his wife just outside the back door, and recall hearing her cry, "He was in jail last night. Now what's he done?"

But I wasn't paying attention. I stood there looking down at two blue, saucer-size plates lying on the dirty kitchen table. On each one, carefully centered, was pasted a small color print of Sallman's head of Christ. A hole had been punched in the rim of each plate, and a yellow ribbon tied through it so it could be hung on the wall as a plaque.

The kids must have brought them home from Bible school!

I looked at Eli and his brother, their noses pressed tight against the window as they looked out into the dark alley.

Then I opened the kitchen door and followed their father to the squad car.

INSTANT CITY

SOUND:	ROLLING DRUMS—HIT IN HARD—END ABRUPTLY
RAY:	Friends, this is no ordinary sale of land.
BOB:	That's right. We're not going to enter into pushy recitals about a piece of desert acreage that will be skyrocketing in value because of the ocean soon to be built there . . .
RAY:	. . . Or about fabulous plans to build a 7,000-room luxury motel right on the shores of that brand-new modern ocean.
BOB:	That's storybook stuff. Nonsense.
RAY:	We're not knocking fly-by-night real-estate operators. They've got to make a killing, too.
BOB:	But those swindlers are doing it the wrong way.
RAY:	You see, in order to start a prosperous community, you need the *people* there first . . . not the land. And the more people you get, the more prosperity there will be for all.
BOB:	That's where we come in. We can get you all the people you need to start a typical community . . . before a single building, ocean, golf-course, highway, school or planned recreation center is built.

From a Bob and Ray Broadcast.

RAY: We have the answer right here—it's the Bob and Ray Portable Collapsible Picket Fence, guaranteed to start a new city.

BOB: Properly used, this item can bring in enough people to start a city the size of Pittsburgh, overnight. And here's the way it works . . .

SOUND: WIND, AS THOUGH ACROSS A PRAIRIE—SOFTLY IN—RAISE—THEN DOWN AND UNDER

RAY: Go to the bleakest, most uninhabitable spot in this country of ours. When you get there, open the Bob and Ray Portable Collapsible Picket Fence to its full dimensions . . . four feet high, seven feet long . . . and anchor the end-poles into the ground.

BOB: Then get behind the Bob and Ray Portable Collapsible Picket Fence . . . and stay there.

RAY: That's all there is to it.

BOB: Within a few seconds, a person will appear out of nowhere. He'll look over the top of the fence and ask you what you are doing.

RAY: Say nothing. The person will leave . . .

BOB: . . . And in half an hour, he'll be back with two friends. *They* will ask you what you are doing.

RAY: Say nothing. They will go. Do not abandon your position behind the fence.

SOUND: AUTO TRAFFIC—SNEAK IN AND HOLD LOW

BOB: You won't have long to wait. In very short order, you'll hear some automobiles pulling up to the fence. The occupants will shout from the cars . . . ask you what you are doing.

RAY: Don't answer. One of the automobiles will leave and begin to bring in carloads of people. Already there is taxi service.

SOUND: RAISE AUTO TRAFFIC AND HOLD MEDIUM

BOB: Competition being what it is, another car will start operating as a taxi, at a lower rate.

RAY: Stay out of it . . . stay behind your fence. There's lots going on out there.

SOUND: ADD NOISE OF CROWD TALKING

BOB: That's right. People are flooding the area at a fantastic rate. The taxis have been replaced by more practical buses.

SOUND: AIR HAMMERS AND RIVETING—HOLD MEDIUM THEN UNDER

RAY: People who prefer to walk have paved the area.

BOB: . . . And several office buildings have been erected so that people will know where they're walking to. By now, many are driving their *own* cars to work.

RAY: By this time, there are homes, shopping areas, an airport, a mayor, and a major league ball club.

BOB: And still the people continue to pour in. New problems are being created.

RAY: Problems of a new city.

BOB: Transportation's a headache. There's a population shift to the suburbs, the reform party has impeached the mayor, slums are developing and there aren't enough teachers for the million and a half school children.

RAY:	A large park has been built around you and your fence . . . the same fence you were crouching behind during the morning hours.
MUSIC	SNEAK IN AND HOLD LOW
BOB:	But now, the first shadows of night are falling over the new city.
RAY:	This is the time for you to pick up your Bob and Ray Portable Collapsible Picket Fence and get out of the park . . .
BOB:	. . . before you're mugged.
RAY:	Literature is available on the fence.
BOB:	Address your cards to "Start A City," and mail them in today.
MUSIC	BRING UP THEN FADE AS ANNOUNCER COMES IN

ANNOUNCER: Bob and Ray's story is true; only the time has been changed. In fact, we can think of only one thing they left out:

Just about the time taxi service starts, a minister will drive up and start holding open-air services. When enough people have gathered, they'll all pitch in and put up a small church building.

As more people try to crowd into the church, a Christian education unit and a larger sanctuary will be added. Soon the church will be a large, imposing structure.

Then, just about the time you're folding up your picket fence, with the sun peering over the horizon and the danger of muggings increasing, the congregation will jack up the building, put wheels under it, and tow it off to a "better" part of town!

As the population of the United States mushrooms and as more and more people move from the country into the city, our metropolitan areas are getting more crowded and more troublesome. Cities that have taken two hundred years to reach their present state will double in size in the next ten or fifteen years. By 1980, say the experts (not Bob and Ray, but the people who study city growth), half of the United States and Canadian population will live in a score of gigantic "strip cities."

These strip cities are solid stretches of close-packed urban development, like the one already reaching down the east coast from Boston to Washington, D.C., or the one now developing between Cincinnati and Detroit.

Just sixty years ago the population of the United States was 76 million, and only 40 per cent of those people lived in cities. Now it is over 180 million, and nearly 75 per cent live in cities.

Meanwhile, the existing cities are changing rapidly. Slum clearance and redevelopment programs wipe out whole sections and then fill the space with new buildings. Huge highways cut paths through the cities, making it easier for commuters to get to the new suburban developments that spring up.

Automation threatens the jobs of thousands of city dwellers. Families scatter across the country and no longer have a patch of ground to call home.

Here are some of the problems this all creates:

Homes—We are not building new city homes, especially low-priced ones, fast enough to accommodate the people who need them. There are not enough apartment units for those city dwellers who prefer to live downtown. And we are not keeping up the existing houses. All this means that people are forced to live in homes less desirable than they would choose, with less room, with scarce neighborhood facilities. It means that many young people live in an environment their parents recognize as unhealthy, but which they can't do anything about.

Schools—The nation is spending about $2 billion less than it should be spending on new schools for the growing cities, while in the heart of town the old schools are falling apart. This means overcrowded classrooms, overworked teachers, and poor education.

Churches—Protestant denominations need thousands of new congregations every year to keep up with population growth, but they aren't coming anywhere near this. In fact, many downtown churches have moved to the suburbs; thus, while the downtown city population in the United States has stayed the same (about 50 million in the last two censuses) the number of churches available to serve them has dropped sharply.

The denominations are concerned about finding ways to meet the special needs of city dwellers. The city environment seems to be harder on people than life in the country.

It's a sad fact of city life that most dealings with other persons are impersonal and shallow. City dwellers know one another as fragments of persons, not as whole people. For example, a city housewife will buy groceries regularly from eight or nine different people in several stores, and not know one of them as well as a rural housewife knows the man who runs the general store. People are not bound together by common loyalties and acquaintances, nor do they seem to care much about one another's lives.

Real friendships make up a much smaller portion of the city man's acquaintanceship than it does for the country man. This life of a multitude of passing, partial acquaintanceships may be what makes many city dwellers frustrated and tense.

The denominations are concerned, too, about the way cities are being planned. Too many are being projected only in terms of brick and steel, rather than in concern for the human lives which will be spent there. And where once the church was at the very heart of town from its founding, now zoning ordinances are setting up standards under which churches will be "allowed" in certain areas.

Christians are also concerned about the 100 million unreached persons in our land, many of whom claim church loyalty but take no part in any church activity. There is concern for such persons as the migrant city dwellers, the elderly, the single adults, the divorced, and the widowed. They are our brothers, but we hardly know them—much less help them. When will concern be translated into concrete action?

In the suburbs, where many new Protestant churches are being built, pastors are worried about the fact that church membership makes so little impact on the people who come. They come swarming in, because belonging to a church is the "normal" thing nowadays. But their basic values, their morals, the way they look at life often seem to be determined more by magazine ads and business practices than by the Scriptures.

So the Church looks at the changing cities and asks, "How long can we Christians go on in the same old way while the world is changing?"

MORE OF
EVERYTHING

THE SEASON WAS SPRING, the month May, but the soft
night was early summer. From where she sat on the
tenement roof, Maria Nunez looked off toward Central Park
and saw the bright windows and irregular patches of light.
It had been a short climb from the fire escape up the ladder
to the roof, and she had avoided unnecessary conversation
with her father, mother, two uncles, two aunts, and several
family friends, all crowded into the little kitchen with its
one window.

Overhead the sky was prodigal with stars, and thin, tenu-
ous clouds had been torn apart by the passage of the moon.
She had come to the roof at dusk to admire the tops of
buildings less than a mile away, but separated by a greater
distance than she had come a week before.

Night had come slowly to the city, to obliterate the form,
thrust, and strength of the monoliths, to tone down the
burnished metal and stone of intricate design, to erase the
towers, and bring patterns of color into tier after tier of
windows. People lived differently in such rich, marvelous
buildings, and with her chin supported by the palm of her
hand, Maria wondered in what luxury they bathed and
dressed. How different were the streets below; not at all
like Puerto Rico where the houses were little more than

From the novel, *West Side Story*, by Irving Shulman based on the Broad-
way musical of the same name.

hovels without floors, without glass in the windows, and certainly without plumbing. Most of the streets were unpaved, without sidewalks, and poverty was everywhere.

When she had been met only the week before at the airport, she had had to blink and make certain that the man and woman running toward her with outstretched arms were her parents, for they appeared so much younger, more self-assured, even better dressed than she had last seen them two years before. At the time they had migrated to New York, it had been decided that she and her sisters would remain behind with relatives. Only Bernardo, her brother, would accompany them to New York until they could get themselves established.

Her father had frowned and not replied when she asked why Bernardo hadn't come to the airport. But she soon knew the reason. He was eighteen and handsome; but his eyes were too bitter, his mouth too tight, his voice too high, and every word he spoke dripped hatred of Americans.

They had more here in New York, more of everything, even of hatred; and to be rid of the latter Maria would have given up everything else and returned to Puerto Rico because she believed it was wrong to hate. She didn't want to hate when it was so much more wonderful to love.

Maria yawned, stretched her arms and wondered if she ought to go to sleep. She might go down and study English grammar or practice speaking English with her father and try to remember that in this language verbs were placed differently in sentences. But the kitchen was filled with company and they were probably talking about San Juan and the little community they had once called home. Why had they left Puerto Rico? This they need not answer, for they had only to touch their pockets and look at the kitchen sink with its faucets.

Winking lights cut diagonally across the city, and Maria followed that flight. Was this plane coming from Puerto Rico? Was it returning to Puerto Rico? Again she was tempted to return to the kitchen, but everyone there would be speaking in Spanish, and if they spoke English it would sound like Spanish. She wanted to speak English as Americans did, with harsh consonants and clipped vowels and no music or lilt in their speech. She wanted so much to be an American.

Maria stood to stretch her arms and embrace the moon and stars. Yesterday she had been sixteen and her mother had kissed her many times as she exclaimed what a beautiful bride Maria would be. And Chino Martin, Bernardo's friend, had looked at her with eyes filled with love. Later he had spoken to Bernardo and to her parents about wanting to marry her. He was a steady boy and worked as an apprentice in a dress factory on Seventh Avenue; some day he would be a full-fledged union operator. Chino was good looking, very shy, much different from Bernardo.

Standing on her toes, moving about, Maria whirled and kissed her hands at the sky and the distant towers. If she married Chino her sisters would have more room because she and Chino would have a flat of their own. And if they made love, it would be more wonderful because they would have the privacy on the day they were married that her mother and father had not known for almost twenty years. Maria covered her face. She had to stop thinking such things, even when she was alone on the roof and in love with the world.

30

Did it include Chino Martin? She wasn't quite sure. Yes, she loved him as she loved everything in the world, but no more than that.

She heard the heavy metal door to the roof open and turned to see the dark shadow of a man. A startled flash of fear vanished at the sound of her name, and her respondent sigh of relief was loud enough to tell Bernardo she had recognized him.

"How come you're sitting on the roof alone?" Bernardo challenged his sister.

"Why not?" she asked him.

"Because it isn't safe," he said. "Not even if you were sitting up here with Anita."

"Why not?" Maria persisted in this question. "Isn't Anita your girl?"

"I guess so," Bernardo said. Resting against the parapet, he lit a cigarette, flicked the match toward the street, and watched the path of its descent. "It isn't safe to sit on a roof alone. There's too many bums in this neighborhood. If one of those Jets saw you sitting up here no telling what might happen."

Despite the night's warmth, Maria trembled. "Would one of them have done . . . that?"

"Without thinking twice," Bernardo replied, then dragged hard at the cigarette. "One of them threw a stink bomb into Guerra's grocery tonight. If I catch him he won't have any arms left."

"You know the boy who did it?"

"What's the difference? He was a Jet. The first one we catch is going to be the first one to get it. If they catch one of us, we get it."

MARIA STOOD TO STRETCH HER ARMS AND EMBRACE THE MOON AND STARS.

"But why should it be this way?" Maria asked her brother. "Why should they hurt us?"

"Because they say we hurt them by coming here. You know what I'm going to do?"

"What?"

"Maybe tomorrow, I'm going down to Times Square with

a couple of the boys—Pepe, Anxious, Toro, and Moose. And
we're going into one of them souvenir stores."

"To rob it?" Maria was frightened.

Bernardo stroked his sister's cheek. "Of course not," he
said. "Just to buy some iron statues of the Statue of Liberty.
Some of them come about this long"—he indicated a meas-

urement of about twelve inches—"and they'd be just about the right size for beating in the head of those Jets. You know what it says on the Statue of Liberty?" he challenged his sister.

"No," she replied. "Should I?"

"It says something about all the poor people coming here to find a better life. Well maybe it's true," Bernardo continued, "but the Jets don't believe it. So we got to beat it into their thick heads. And little Statues of Liberty seem just the right way to do it."

Maria stood to confront her brother. Eyes wide, her heart beating so hard it was frightening, she shook her head slowly as she fixed the knot of Bernardo's tie which had slipped to one side of his collar. Her brother was so good looking, but his mouth was too thin, and his eyes were like those of an animal she had once seen in a trap; they were fearful, but defiant in their hatred. His enmity was often unspoken, but more to be feared than noisy rage.

"Why must it be this way?" she said. "These people," she moved her arm to encompass the city, "I don't hate them."

"But they don't love you," Bernardo replied. "Look," he was impatient, "I don't want you on the roof alone."

Maria wiped at her eyes, "Not even with Chino?"

"Not even with Chino," her brother replied.

"But he likes me," she said. "Is it true really, that he spoke to mamma and pappa—about marrying me?"

"It's true," Bernardo embraced his sister and crushed her to him. "After you're a bride, you can be alone with Chino.

"Don't go anyplace by yourself," Bernardo warned again.

"The lousy Americans think they're entitled to more than we are, and if they see a girl like you . . ." He paused, stepped back, cocked his head and looked at his sister. "Man, you are one sweet chick. Chino's a lucky fellow. By the way, Maria, you know that he loaned mamma and pappa the money for your fare? Even paid the fare for one of the kids? You know that?"

Maria bowed her head. "I know that. So I must work hard at my job to earn enough money to pay it back."

"But you like him?"

"Yes," Maria said.

Bernardo crushed the butt under his foot and removed a fresh cigarette from the pack. "How about loving him?"

"I don't know," Maria said. "But he's a nice boy."

"Let's get off the roof." Bernardo took his sister's hand. "The company's gone and you can go to sleep. By the way, I forgot to ask you. How do you like your new job?"

"I love it," Maria clapped her hands. "Imagine, working in a bridal shop! The dresses, the veils, everything is so beautiful."

"You'll be the prettiest bride," Bernardo said to his sister. "The most beautiful of them all. When Chino sees you coming down the aisle it'll just knock him out. Maybe he's not like the other Sharks, because he's got a job and goes to work. But I wouldn't want any of the other Sharks for you." He opened the roof door for his sister and bowed gracefully. "Si, he'll make you a good husband, Maria. So you ought to try to fall in love with him."

"I'll try, Bernardo," she promised. "I'll try with all my heart. Are you going to sleep now too?"

"Later," Bernardo said. "I've got to see some of the boys."

"About what?" Maria asked. "To go fighting?"

Bernardo kissed his sister's cheek. "Just to talk things over." He was evasive.

"God go with you," she said.

"Sure," Bernardo replied. "I don't care if He comes along."

* * * * *

Maria is just one of more than 700,000 Puerto Ricans crowded into sections of New York City. Most of them have come since World War II, trying to find a better life than the one back home. Hundreds land daily at Idlewild Airport.

A high percentage of them are Roman Catholic, of course, but there are surprising numbers of Protestants. Astonished researchers recently discovered during a religious survey that some 250 independent Protestant Spanish-speaking churches have sprung up in New York City's Puerto Rican neighborhoods.

More than 32,000 people belong to these churches, and another 13,600 belong to churches of sixteen regular denominations, operated with the help of the New York City Mission Society.

People meet special problems in ministering to these strangers who are their brothers. For example, there is a question whether worship should be conducted in Spanish, which most people understand best, or in English, which they should be encouraged to learn if they hope to adjust to the rest of society.

And the Puerto Rican youth often meet special problems. Constantly facing prejudice and fighting poverty, and forced to live in overcrowded areas because they aren't allowed elsewhere, they show their resentment in ways that society doesn't approve. They may end up in gangs, in courts, in jail.

The churches, the "Y's" and the city police are all trying to help these frustrated, confused youth.

One of the main things all three try to do, according to David W. Barry, executive director of the New York City Mission Society, is to convince young people "that another way of life is not only better, but possible. The delinquent youth I have known almost invariably are young people who feel trapped, frustrated, resentful, because life confronts them with such major barriers to achievement as racial restrictions, impossible parents, inferior education.

"There is no point in hortatory sermons in such situations; there is much point in programs that patiently seek with young people the doors to achievement."

Church groups have found success in sending youth workers out of the churches to make friends, honestly gain the confidence of gang members, and then show the youth how much advantage there is in "going social"—turning the gang into a constructive club.

Dr. Barry points out that "fundamentally the job of the church working with teen-agers in areas of high delinquency is no different from the church's responsibility to teen-agers anywhere. It is a job of Christian nurture and of calling for commitment to Jesus Christ and his way of life."

Another effective way of doing this has been a series of co-ed conferences, involving several hundred youth from high-delinquency areas at one time.

A worker in the snack bar where one such conference was held complained that many delegates were smoking

TIME . . . THERE'S LOTS OF TIME.
TIME FILLED WITH DESPAIR, HATRED,
HOPELESSNESS. THE PAST IS A DEAD
WEIGHT. THE FUTURE IS TOO DREARY,
TOO UNPROMISING TO PREPARE FOR.
THE PRESENT IS A TIME OF
WAITING—AND HANGING AROUND.

three packs of cigarettes a day. A careful watch had to be
kept for smuggled liquor. And one visitor, not warned of
what to expect, admitted that she was actually scared by
the dress, behavior, and speech of the young delegates.

Yet the workers thought it was a wonderful thing that
the youth were there at all! Dr. Barry says these may be
the only church youth conferences in which most of the
delegates "have direct and personal experience with the
courts, where discussions come around to such questions
as practical methods of resisting rape and what to do when
your father comes at you with a baseball bat. . . ."

Already cynical and disillusioned at the deal the world has given them, these youth have somehow been persuaded to give the Church a chance. What would you say to a group like this, to convince them the Church has an answer?

On the following pages is what José Antonio Morales, former director of youth at the Presbyterian Church of the Crossroads, a church that ministers to Puerto Ricans in New York, told such a conference group.

He had to use simple words, and he could give only a narrow definition, but he got across part of the answer to their question, "What is a church?"

WHAT IS A CHURCH?

WHAT IS MY CHURCH? What is your church? Yesterday a young man in a discussion group said that his was a place to pray in.

I wonder how many of us would agree with him, that the church is a place where Christians go to take part in a worship service or a mass or a prayer meeting; that it's a large room where a minister or a priest gets up once a week and tells us to be good and talks about the Bible in a way we don't understand; that it's a place where these long, drawn-out talks are the most important things that happen during the week.

If all of this is so, then Sunday is the only day in which our church is doing anything and maybe during the other six days the place should be closed.

I mention these points because the church has been all these things to me, boring, dull, uninteresting, and the Bible a pretty sad book.

Aha, you say, here it comes, now he's going to tell us what the church means to him now. He's going to say how the church has changed him and how he's a new man because of it. He's going to say that he listens to all the sermons and understands all of the Bible readings perfectly.

Well, I'll say this, that at Crossroads we don't have organ

Part of a talk given by José Antonio Morales, former Youth Director at the Presbyterian Church of the Crossroads, New York City.

IS THIS THE CHURCH—A PLACE WHERE YOU WORSHIP?

pipes to count but I can tell you how many light bulbs there are in each fixture. Sometimes I can't be reached by the sermon either and so I count the light bulbs.

Well, then, why do you go to church, you say. Why are

you going to tell us to go and support the church with our time, our money, our attendance?

Because, I'll say, the church is more than the sermon on Sunday and the prayer meeting during the week. Because the church, my church, your church, stands for a way of life which by the example of Jesus Christ is the perfect way.

The same young man who said that the church was a place to pray also said something else—that this particular church with a community center in it was separate from the community center. "The Center's a place to play, man, and that's what you do there."

Well what about this? Why did the church decide to put a center in anyway? Because kids need a place to play? What about public schools, P.A.L., Boys' Clubs? Don't they provide a place to play?

Or is it that there is something special about that church with the beat-up gyms and the no-dancing, no-smoking rules? What about the *people* in that church community house, are they different? Do they take a different kind of interest in you?

Let's look at this church community center further. In it we find a housing clinic to help people get better housing. We also find language classes so that people who want to learn to speak English can do it free of charge. We find crafts classes, club group meetings, basketball games, and Boy Scouts, and they send kids away to camp.

Is all of this just to fill in the time between Sundays?

When a kid is on probation, why does a church worker go to see his probation officer? When he goes on trial, why does the minister or the priest or the worker go to court with him? When the family loses one of its members, why

OR IS THE CHURCH AT THE SINK, THE LATHE, THE
BLACKBOARD, THE DESK, THE WHEEL OF YOUR CAR?

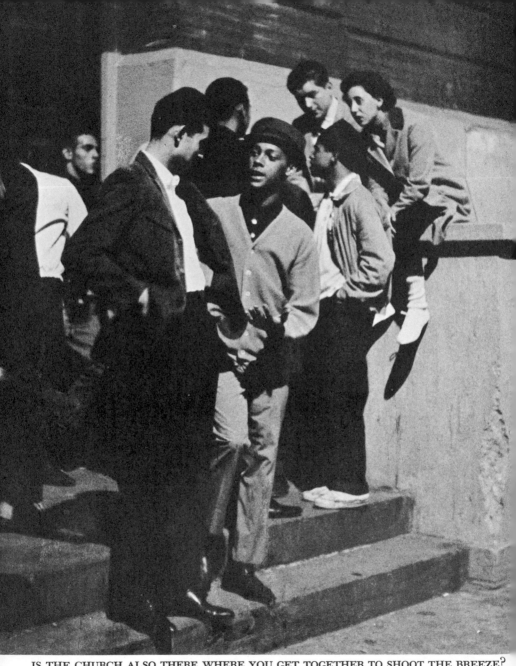

IS THE CHURCH ALSO THERE WHERE YOU GET TOGETHER TO SHOOT THE BREEZE?

does the church concern itself with the family even after the burial?

What I'm really asking is, do you realize that this, too, is part of your church's work? And do you realize that all of the concern which the church expresses for you is part of the job laid out for it by Jesus Christ?

You know, Jesus was concerned about people in need and if he were alive today, he would be going to court with a young person in trouble and trying to help a junkie kick his habit and trying to keep two clubs from fighting.

This is the life which he is asking us to lead and that is why our churches are so interested in all of you.

It's good, you say, but, man, when you get back home, it's not so easy. When a guy keeps beating on you and you know that the Bible says that you should love your enemy, it's hard to do. You have to punk out or fight and it's not easy to punk out.

Let me ask you this: Which is harder, to fight or to punk out? Are you taking the easy way when you punk out, or the hard way? You know, the Bible tells you what you should do; it says to turn the other cheek; it says, Don't fight.

Is this the easy way to go? It is full of difficult decisions like the one we've just mentioned. And this is what the church is talking about.

East Harlem, Lower East Side, Bronx, Brooklyn—anywhere you live you'll find people having to make important decisions and you'll find them depending on their church.

The church is very much in the picture, it is very much the place where you and I ought to be, because it is the place that really talks about things that matter.

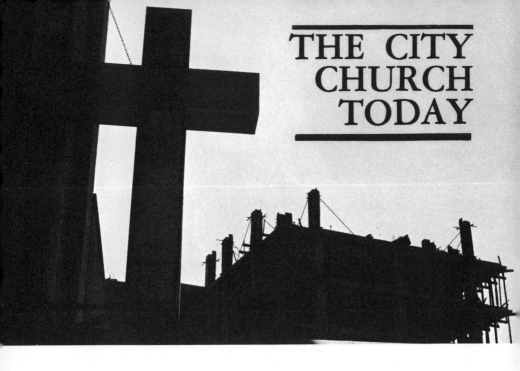

THE CITY CHURCH TODAY

A<small>RE THE</small> <small>CHURCHES</small> meeting the challenge of the changing cities?

The answer seems to be a loud "No!"

Here are some facts to think about:

In Detroit, while the downtown Protestant population has increased over a fifteen-year period, some fifty-five downtown churches have closed, merged, or moved to the suburbs. Forty years ago there were forty-four Lutheran churches within two miles of the downtown area. Now there are four.

In Boston, five downtown Methodist churches have closed in ten years. In Washington, D.C., fourteen Methodist churches have left the second precinct, a depressed area, in twenty years.

Nearly a hundred churches of one denomination in New York City have been abandoned or merged out of existence in a hundred years.

In Philadelphia, twenty downtown Presbyterian churches have moved to the suburbs or closed their doors. In Chicago, there are no Episcopal churches left in the busy "Loop" area.

These are just examples; nearly every denomination in every large city could report similar statistics. And all the time, the number of people needing a ministry in these areas has remained constant or even grown!

Why is this happening? There are many answers:

The exodus to the suburbs. Life in the suburbs has been sold to us as the American dream; many city people move out to them just as soon as they are financially able. Often their decision to move is hastened by the fact that lower-class whites, or Negroes of any class, are beginning to move into the old neighborhood.

When this happens—and it may be a slow process, taking twenty years, or it may happen in six months—the churches of such a neighborhood face real problems. Should they move out where their members now live? If they do, who will minister to those who have come into the community? If the church tries to stay, will it be able to interest the new residents? Many churches move out.

Urban redevelopment. These slum-clearing projects are going on all over the country. Tall apartment buildings go up in the cleared area, but apartment dwellers are hard to reach for the church. In many apartment houses, clergymen aren't allowed to make calls. And the people who live in apartments often are people who don't want to be involved in the affairs of others. This limits their interest in the church.

People on the move. City people move more often. Some city pastors report their membership lists may change 50 per cent in a year. Thus a church that was founded in a stable community fifty years ago may suddenly find that it not only is hard to reach new people, but that these new people leave in six months and the church has to start all over. This has proved too hard for some congregations.

Americanization. Many older downtown churches were formed by groups of immigrants who wanted to preserve the customs of the old country. Now, however, the first generation is mostly gone; the children usually live elsewhere and are thoroughly Americanized. Chances are the neighborhood has changed, bringing in a different racial or ethnic group. The church's original reason for existence has disappeared, and it will die unless a new, sounder reason for existence is found. Many churches just close up.

Real estate. It is easier to raise money for bricks than for staff members, and many downtown churches have poured money into huge imposing structures. Often, members who have a strong sense of loyalty drive in from the suburbs to attend these churches, but tend to ignore the needs of the people around the building.

G. Paul Musselman, in an article about the churches' failure in the cities, tells about one hard-pressed downtown church that strained its budget to build a new educational unit, but fired two parish workers to balance the account.

Sooner or later such churches, walled off from the communities in which they are built, find the suburban faithful dying off or losing their enthusiasm. Membership tapers off, and the building is usually sold—at a big loss—to a congregation of people who live in the neighborhood.

Finances. Churches that make an honest attempt to stay and serve sometimes find it impossible to maintain building and staff. It takes about five hundred inner-city members to equal the giving of two hundred suburban members, and sometimes the church just can't grow that big. Here is where the suburban churches could have a real mission, sharing the financial burden with the struggling inner-city congregation. All too often, however, the suburbanites are more concerned with their new $300,000 education unit than with what looks like a hopeless struggle downtown.

It would not be fair, however, to say that every church is running away from the inner-city's problems.

The story of one church that dared to stay—and still is facing problems—begins on page 103 of this book. There are scores of others.

New York Avenue Presbyterian Church in Washington is one. This was the church whose pastor was the late Dr. Peter Marshall, Chaplain of the Senate and subject of the movie, *A Man Called Peter.* Nine presidents, including Lincoln, have worshiped there.

After World War II the church found itself on the edge of the second precinct, scene of Washington's heaviest concentration of Negro families. Fancy brownstone houses, once the homes of wealthy and influential church members, now were crowded by as many as a dozen families, one family to a room.

The church decided to stay and witness to its community, although it would have been easy to move to the suburbs along with the majority of its members.

Staying meant inheriting problems of alcoholism, race tension, juvenile delinquency, and broken homes.

But New York Avenue is reaching people in the area. Sunday church school classes and social groups in the church are mobilized to work with neighborhood residents, not only to make them a part of the church but also to help them take advantage of the various government and city agencies that can help them have a better community.

The church hopes to establish six store front missions within the area, since an imposing church building often scares away potential members in such a neighborhood.

Already New York Avenue church is anticipating another change: the whole neighborhood will be part of a slum clearance project and will eventually be a neighborhood of middle-class apartments. This means an entirely different ministry, but the church is determined to stay and serve.

Another Washington church, Augustana Lutheran, started as a church for Swedish immigrants. It has weathered not only the Americanization of its neighborhood, but also an influx that makes half the area Negro. At the end of the war most of its members lived in the suburbs of Maryland and Virginia; it would have been easy for the church to move out.

But Augustana Lutheran stayed, pounded on doors, adjusted its program to the interests of people in the neighborhood, and has grown from 350 to 600 members, including 100 Negroes.

McCarty Memorial Christian Church in Los Angeles was established years ago in an all-white neighborhood, but in twenty years the area became almost entirely Negro. Many churches pulled out, selling their buildings to Negro congregations.

McCarty Memorial stayed. When the first church-sponsored party for youth of the neighborhood had to be chaperoned by police, members had some second thoughts about their decision. But the police aren't necessary any more; the teen-agers have learned a real sense of responsibility in the church, which carries over into their life in the community.

Ministering to an inner-city community usually involves such concerns as working for better housing, police protection, and graft-free politics. The Rev. James E. Gusweller, an Episcopal minister to Puerto Ricans on Manhattan's upper west side, has clashed with landlords who charge high rents for slum rooms without toilets or running water.

He tried to find out how the landlords could get away with violating housing ordinances by the dozen, and made headlines by exposing housing inspectors who were taking bribes to overlook the violations. He even hauled some landlords into court when they refused to obey the law.

Even in areas where many congregations have fled, the church is making a comeback with a new type of program. In the second precinct of Washington, mentioned earlier, there's an "S.O.S." program—"Shepherds of the Streets." Wesley Theological Seminary and the Methodist churches surrounding the precinct sponsor this ministry.

The South End Methodist Parish ministers to gangs in a tough section of Boston, helping them find a better reason for existence than fighting. The Mid-town Methodist Parish in Philadelphia meets needs of the people ranging all the way from learning to cook to studying the meaning of Holy Communion.

First Church of the Brethren in Chicago has Negro, Latin-American, Chinese, and Caucasian faces in its congregation each Sunday. It ministers to youth in an area where the Vice Lords and the Cobras, two of Chicago's largest gangs, roam the streets at night.

Cleveland has an inner-city interdenominational parish like those in Chicago and East Harlem; plans are being made to start one in Indianapolis.

New battle plans are being drawn up everywhere in the fight for the city church. In Detroit, city-wide planning may result in the closing of some churches in order that others may have sufficient staff to serve the area.

Some leaders say Protestant churches should adopt the Roman Catholic idea of the parish—a definite geographical area for which a given congregation is responsible. The pastor would be told that this, and this alone, was his field. He was to know every person in the area, and be the pastor of each one whether he responds or not.

This, it is argued, would stop competition among Protestant churches in an overchurched area. And it would eliminate the temptation to move the church out to the suburbs. The church would be the church of the neighborhood, not of a scattered membership.

Other ways of adapting to the changing community are being tried. In Houston, Texas, St. Stephen's Episcopal Church found itself surrounded by new apartments in which the pastor got a chilly reception. So the parish was divided into twenty "zones," each of which set up a series of discussion groups led by laymen. People can get involved and feel they belong in these smaller groups, to an extent that would be unlikely in a larger congregation.

Pastor John Gensel of Manhattan's Advent Lutheran Church recognizes the hours his city people keep by scheduling a service at 5 P.M. Much of his calling is in coffee houses, bars, and clubs; he has helped jazz musicians, entertainers, and other "night people" discover that the church is honestly concerned for them as persons.

The inner-city ministry, as you can see, involves much more than opening the church doors and preaching a good sermon once a week.

But the Rev. Julius H. Belser of Chicago's West Side Christian Parish (described more fully on page 79) has reminded us that physical improvements in the inner-city are only a beginning.

In a sermon to a suburban Illinois congregation, he said:

"The Christian hope is the complete assurance that in Christ God has, and will, overcome the world.

"We must be very careful that we do not offer our people jobs, activities, influence, respectability without new life in Christ Jesus."

Is the church meeting the challenge? Yes and no. The number of churches that run still exceed those that stay. The number of suburban churches that are unconcerned with the spiritual needs of their brethren in the inner-city still are greater than those willing to send money and spend time there.

But there is a new spirit of urgency, of adventure, in the church's concern for the cities. We are beginning to see that every church is responsible for what happens in every community. We *are* brothers, and if we are still strangers, it is part of our work as Christians to break down the barriers between us.

YOU DON'T SEE THEM ANY MORE

Hughie McCarron came to the end of his days in a familiar ghost town.

His leonine old head held high in proud defiance against a changing world, he moved up Eighth Avenue each morning on the same solitary walk. Past the crumbling tenements with the boarded up windows.

Past rundown rooming houses with shades drawn discreetly on their aging vices. Past the chili joint, tattoo parlor and pizza palace.

Past the newsstand at the corner of 49th St. where he always paused for a chat with Lenny Mahan, the crippled news dealer who was the last of his friends.

Past the big marquee jutting out from the solid mass of Madison Square Garden with its promise of crowds and excitement. Past a gaping hole where a bulldozer dug into the rubble of an old brownstone that had housed some of his closest cronies.

That was only yesterday. But, in the quicksilver life of a big city, it was long, long ago.

All his life, Hughie McCarron fought against moving away from the old neighborhood. He never could bring himself to realize that the old neighborhood was moving away from him; that each day the familiar streets grew emptier of the faces and sites he had known since boyhood.

From an Associated Press release written by Hugh Mulligan.

So when he died at 82 in the loneliness of a furnished room, the only one to minister to him was a man he hadn't spoken to in 16 years because of some dimly remembered petty grievance.

His last trip across town, to the morgue at Bellevue, was at public expense in a city ambulance. This, too, was ironic, because Hughie McCarron was an independent soul who had worked hard in life and at the end, proudly scorned welfare assistance.

No one bothered to claim the estate. It consisted only of a $12 radio, a safety razor, one pair of bifocals, a set of false teeth, two subway tokens and a frayed but carefully brushed overcoat.

No one bothered to claim the body. Before Lenny Mahan and the boys around the Garden caught up with him, his remains had been shipped to the Cornell medical center for dissection by medical students.

In a city of 7,781,984 people, in the rush and roar of the world's most exciting metropolis, Hughie McCarron had led a lonely life; a stranger in the midst of millions, a lost soul shrinking into oblivion within a few blocks of the Great White Way.

He was only one of many. There are thousands like him: the lonely people of the big cities. His story is repeated endlessly in New York, Chicago, in Philadelphia, in San Francisco, in Cleveland, the big bustling cities where life belongs to the young and eager, and a lonely death awaits the old and the forsaken. The years drop steadily from the calendar, but the months, the days, the hours drag on in a monotony of aimless wandering through the familiar streets of a busy ghost town.

You see the lonely old folks at suppertime in the downtown cafeterias, spooning out life's remaining hours in driblets of pathetic ceremony. Only the lonely know how to stretch a meal to the brink of eternity. Half an hour over the fruit juice. Another half hour over the soup and crackers. An hour over the swiss steak or chicken croquettes.

Not long ago in Jackson Heights, one of New York's jampacked apartment house districts, an elderly man lay down on the tracks of the elevated railway to die. He had $10,000 in the bank, he told the officer who thwarted his plans, and didn't know a soul in the entire city. Why go on?

But most of them do.

Last year the public administrator in Manhattan, which is only one of the city's five boroughs, padlocked the homes, the apartments, the flats, the furnished rooms of some five thousand New Yorkers who had died unattended and without known heirs.

Relatives eventually came forth to claim the estates of all but five hundred of these. The average estate was slightly under $4,000, mostly in life insurance. Just enough to pay the funeral expenses, satisfy back bills and perhaps secure a headstone to mark the uncertain passage of another stranger through the crowded streets.

Modern medicine had prolonged their lives, but modern society hadn't quite figured out why. New homes in the suburbs were too tidy, too compact to provide room for an aging grandfather or grandmother; the new efficiency apartments too efficient to tolerate any form of decrepitude.

You see them sunning themselves on the benches in the park, or feeding pigeons in a public square. You see them hovering over excavation sites, hypnotized by Manhattan's

SOMETIMES I GET TO THINKING ABOUT
THE DAYS WHEN I WAS USEFUL. . . .

THERE ARE A LOT OF US LIKE THIS.
WE'RE A LITTLE OUT OF THINGS; LIFE
GOES ON, BUT WE DON'T SEEM TO MAKE
MUCH DIFFERENCE.

maddest melody, the ceaseless clamor of the jackhammers and riveting guns.

On a bench in Madison Square park, a weathered old man with snow white hair fixed his tired eyes intently on the renovation work in progress on the Metropolitan Life Insurance company building.

"I can remember when that building went up," he announced tentatively, trying not to be too obvious about his desperate need for conversation. "They called it 'The Light That Never Failed.' I guess that's before your time."

His double-breasted suit was a trifle threadbare and, like the too thick knot in his tie, clearly belonged to another

YOU YOUNG FOLKS
DON'T KNOW WHAT IT'S LIKE
TO WORK HARD ALL YOUR LIFE
AND THEN SUDDENLY TO
BE NOTHING.

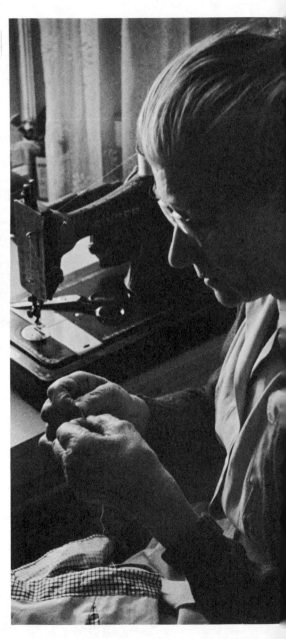

OH, THERE ARE SOME THAT
HAVE SOMETHING TO
LIVE FOR.

generation. But his khaki shirt was clean, if a bit gone at the collar, and there was a shine on his shoes and a jaunty flower in his buttonhole.

He carefully folded his newspaper, lately rescued from a bus seat and stuffed it into a side pocket as insurance against a time when there would be no one to talk to. The lonely have a touching sense of dignity and a keen sense of economics.

You see them on rainy afternoons in the side street residential hotels. In the lonely lobby, swapping the proud little perjuries that time has taught them to believe, "My daughter is always begging me to come live with them, but I wouldn't dream of butting in on her life and the children's."

"On Mother's Day he takes me to a very expensive restaurant and, believe me, the sky's the limit."

In New York, many of the oldsters finish out their days at the Bird S. Coler home on Welfare Island. "Farewell Island," the patients call it, because they know the next step is the grave. Only the lonely know what it's like to spend years, sometimes decades, on a tiny island in the East river, in full view of Manhattan's teeming concrete canyons, and never have a visitor.

In his nineteen years as chaplain on Welfare Island, Father Joseph McGowan, a gentle, silver-haired old Jesuit, has sympathized often with the two recurring nightmares of his dying flock:

"They dread being buried in potter's field and even more than that they dread having their body sent to a medical college. Half of them on this island never expected to come to this kind of an end. They never thought they would die

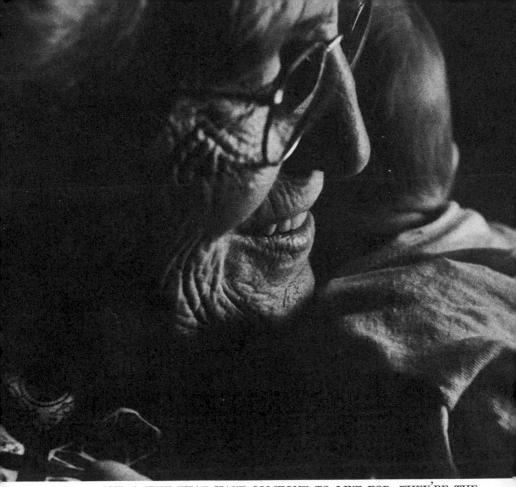

AND A FEW THAT HAVE <u>SOMEONE</u> TO LIVE FOR. THEY'RE THE
LUCKY ONES. BUT HOW MANY DO YOU KNOW LIKE THAT?

friendless and fundless, because at one time they probably
had many friends and plenty of money."

Twelve years ago Father McGowan started St. Joseph's
burial fund to provide a dignified burial in consecrated
ground for many of his indigent parishioners. He has since
buried more than two thousand, mostly Catholics but quite

a few from other faiths, and carefully recorded each name in a little black ledger.

Father McGowan's "book of the dead" includes the name of one "lovely old lady" who spent twenty-five years on the island and never had a visitor. "She put up her hair each day and put on her very best dress, as if she were expecting a dear friend to come through the door at any moment. I used to tell her any man would be proud to be her lover."

He remembers another woman who sat on a bench by the river day after day, repeating over and over: "I have twelve children and here I am."

You see them on winter afternoons in the reading rooms of the public libraries, where the atmosphere is warm and cozy, the chairs big and comfortable, and where there's always someone around to share a sigh for the romances of Faith Baldwin and Joseph C. Lincoln. Only the lonely have really savored the thrills of far-away places and the vicarious companionship of books, the eternal happy endings.

You see them in bus stations and railroad terminals and all-night movie houses. You see them early in the afternoon nursing a beer in the near-empty bars, hoping that the bartender is in a conversational mood and not too busy with other customers.

You see them late at night in deserted churches, lighting a candle for the friends who are gone and the long days ahead. You see them wandering vacant-eyed down strange new streets, uprooted from the old neighborhood in the name of progress.

You see them feeding the ducks in the park pond, or maybe leaving a bit of liverwurst for a stray cat in an alley. And then one day, you don't see them any more.

UP FROM
THE HILLS

WHEN CLETE ALLEN and his family started north for the
city, somebody gave his father a booklet which con-
tained this advice:

> WARNING—You cannot carry shot guns, rifled guns, re-
> volvers, pistols, daggers, straight-edged razors, knucks,
> blackjacks, or switchblade knives. In some states, you can-
> not have guns in your home without a license from the
> police.

It was just one of many things Clete was to find confusing
about the city, from the way police insisted on breaking up
an honest fight to the way the school principal kept trying
to make him attend school even on days when there were
chores to do at home.

But even though he didn't understand it, Clete tried to
make the best of things; he figured they wouldn't be in the
city long anyway.

For Clete was one of America's most unusual group of
changing city residents: people who didn't want to come
there in the first place, and who intend to go back home just
as soon as money makes it possible.

"Home" is the southern mountains—the backwoods hills
and hollows made famous by Snuffy Smith and Li'l Abner.
And Clete is what some sociologists call a "WASP"—a White
Appalachian Southern Protestant who has moved north.

In twenty years, two million white mountaineers have
moved into northern states looking for jobs. (That's three

64

times the number of Puerto Ricans who have moved onto the mainland.)

Between 1950 and 1960 one out of every five residents of the southern Appalachian mountains moved north—more than a million people.

They came because their families were too large for their tiny farms—worn-out land on steep hillsides—to support. And where they settled, problems followed. Just one statistic indicates how big a problem:

In 1960, one-third of all the new pupils who entered the Columbus, Ohio schools came from the southern mountains!

Clete Allen, his parents, and the six brothers and sisters who still live at home occupy two rooms on the third floor of a dirty gray slum house near the heart of one of these northern cities. They've been there eight years now.

Clete's mother, standing on the rickety wooden fire escape that serves as a back porch, can't rightly remember when she was last downtown, although it's only a twenty-minute walk. When the family first came to town, somebody had taken her there, but the revolving doors and escalators in the department stores had terrified her.

Besides, the neighborhood stores supply all her needs, and the people she meets in the neighborhood know and understand her. They all came up from the hills, too.

Four of the children sleep in one room and the other two sleep in the living room with their parents. But the Allen "apartment" is as clean and neat as its age will permit. Stacked around on the old bureau and on a bric-a-brac shelf are pictures of the twelve children; six are grown and raising families of their own. There are some religious plaques, "Jesus Saves" and "The Wages of Sin is Death," along with a satin pillow embroidered "Mother" and "Souvenir of Ft. Sill."

Mrs. Allen admits that on the rent they are paying, and with her husband's good salary as a mechanic, the family could move to a low-cost suburban home. "But we know the people here. No tellin' how we'd make out somewhere else."

The apartment looks barren, she explains, because the family furniture was stored with relatives near Harlan, Kentucky, when they made the move eight years ago. "We never decided to bring it up here; guess I just don't like the city."

The ways he learned back home make plenty of problems for Clete, who's now sixteen years old.

Back home, school wasn't regarded as very important. Only 11 per cent of the rural adults in the hills have as much as twelve years of schooling; in Tennessee it's 13 per cent and in West Virginia 12 per cent.

So when Clete began coming to school only in the afternoon, his mother was called in. "He's got chores to do," she told the principal, "and he's going to do them. I'm bringin' him up right, or I'm moving to where they'll let me."

Clete fought a running battle with the truant officer until he was sixteen, and then dropped out. His parents didn't object. He hadn't enjoyed any part of school; even the extra-curricular activities were too competitive.

Back home, at recess time, you'd see all the kids doing just what their fathers did with leisure time: "just a-settin'." Here, everybody runs around, playing games against somebody, always trying to win, being organized into teams, or troops, or squads.

He didn't like the names he got called at school, either—briarhopper or briar; ridge runner; swamp turkey; or, worst of all, hillbilly.

Clete has already had one brush with the police, too, although he's not vicious or even a trouble-maker.

Back home, a fight was the way to settle an argument. Clete's ancestors were Scotch-Irish settlers who had left the old country because they didn't like the English telling them what to do.

They had always fought their own battles, needing no outsider to help. But here in the city, Clete found, the police try to stop fights, and sometimes even jail a fellow for using a gun or knife. One night, standing around with a group of other young fellows, Clete had been searched by a patrolman, and booked for carrying a concealed switchblade knife.

Clete looks forward to the time when he'll be old enough to hang around the neighborhood bar—a dim, smoky place with the ironic legend, "Briars Welcome" lettered on the window. Back home it had been the general store where the menfolk gathered in the evening to talk and socialize; here the men gather in the bar to laugh, drink, talk about home, and listen to loud juke-box music about the hills.

Four or five times a year the Allen family crowds into the 1949 Ford for a trip back to see the home folk. This is a return to their real roots; in the city they will never be anything but strangers in a foreign land.

On other weekends, family folk from back home visit the city. Crowding another six or eight into the two rooms is no hardship; the strongest ties the mountaineers have is family, and this extends to fifth and sixth cousins.

68

When they aren't visiting or being visited, the Allens may go to church. They usually drive eight miles across town to a Pentecostal church, which used to meet in a nearby abandoned store room, but which now proudly occupies a white cement block building complete with steeple.

They like the church because the preaching and the singing sound so much like what they used to have back home. They went once to the big church on the corner a few blocks from the apartment, but the songs were unfamiliar, and they felt the people there stared at them because of their clothes. They haven't gone back.

City officials and welfare people in the city are concerned about people like the Allens.

They know that the Allen children are not stupid, that they are not naturally dirty, that their parents are not naturally inclined to crime any more than any other group in the city. But the grades of southern mountain children often *are* lower than average; their housing is usually below standard, and the crime rate is higher in the neighborhoods where people like the Allens live.

Officials recognize several things that make this possible.

The mountaineers' lack of education makes it hard for them to find good jobs; some of them end up on relief. Others, too independent for that, drift from city to city, never becoming stable citizens. Some move in with relatives and make overcrowding even worse.

The lack of competitive spirit, typical of life in the mountains, makes it unnatural for the fathers to compete for good jobs and the sons to compete for good grades. And with the low status that education has in the hills, the "dropout" rate among city teen-agers from the mountains is fantastic.

GOD PUT ME ON THE SOFT EARTH . . .

Ignorance about health and sanitation, and a tendency to accept ill health as inevitable, make the mountaineers' neighborhoods a health hazard in the city. One family threw garbage out of the windows; when told that garbage should be wrapped, they wrapped it—and then threw it out of the windows.

The fact that the quality of his housing didn't matter much to the mountaineer when he lived back home, as long as he had a roof, makes the new city dwellers satisfied with the most dismal slum rooms. They often don't care much about fixing up their quarters or moving to better ones.

HARD TIMES PUT ME ON THE PAVEMENT.

The independence that the mountaineer inherited from his Scotch-Irish ancestors, intensified by 150 years of isolation from the rest of the world, makes the southern whites sensitive to criticism, real or imagined. They mistrust everybody they meet in the city who isn't from their part of the country.

This and their lack of respect for the law of "outsiders" make problems not only for the police but for any organization that tries to help them. Neighborhood councils, the P.T.A.'s, the Scouts, the Y's, and even most of the churches sound too regimented.

71

Even the fact that their roots remain back on the south side of the Ohio River is a problem as well as a blessing.

It seems to be good for people, in this day when so many families across the country move every year, to have some place to which the family is strongly tied—a place that will always be "home." Psychologists point out that southern mountaineers in the city seem to have fewer personality disturbances than the average city dweller, and say this solid sense of belonging somewhere is probably the reason.

On the other hand, this allegiance to another home means that the mountaineer tends not to get involved in the life of the city, even though he may live there twenty years. He doesn't join, he doesn't help, because he doesn't intend to stay.

It's not fair to imply that the above impressions are true of every southern mountaineer who has moved to the city. Thousands of them have adapted well to city life, demonstrating ambition to work their way into better jobs, to live in clean, spacious homes, and to take part in community activities.

But there are more than two million of these strangers in the city, and the many who *don't* adjust make real problems for their fellow citizens.

Although Clete and his kinfolk do not necessarily recognize it, they represent a real problem for your church and mine. The fact that they do not feel at home in our churches is a challenge to many Christians, who feel that Christ's church should be able to make them welcome as brothers.

Back home, the mountaineers' churches emphasized heaven and its rewards—a wonderful dawning that would make all present suffering seem as nothing.

This helped the Allens accept things as they were—even poverty, ignorance, and poor health.

The church they attend in the city preaches the same gospel, with no emphasis on what Christians might do to help make the present life richer.

As a matter of fact, the Allens' church actually makes adjustment harder for some people, by forbidding much that is a part of city life, setting them farther apart from their neighbors.

The preaching the Allens hear, both in church and (at full volume) on the radio, features a stern, punishing God. It is understood, however, that most of God's wrath will be unleashed on those who in this life are wealthy, while eternal life will be reserved for the well-behaved poor. There is little emphasis on man's duty to his fellow man— a vital duty for city Christians.

The churches are still searching for ways to minister to people like the Allens, to help them find both a sound spiritual foundation for life and a better adjustment to society.

In Dayton, Ohio, the Methodist church has reopened an abandoned church in the heart of a southern white neighborhood as a community center. A full-time staff of persons who understand and appreciate families like Clete's is living and working in the neighborhood.

In Cincinnati, an Episcopal minister who found the mountaineers flocking into his neighborhood took a sleeping room in a tenement, in order to be closer to them and understand them better.

The churches are also active in the Mayor's Friendly Relations Committee, a Cincinnati group that helps both newcomers and long-time residents understand the problems of adjustment. It publishes pamphlets like the one that warned Clete's father about carrying guns, and holds workshops for community leaders to help change scorn to sympathy for the newcomers.

In Detroit, churches have combined in a person-to-person plan of visitation, repeatedly assuring newcomers that the established church is interested in them.

And youth groups in several of the cities, recognizing the loneliness of young men and women who come up from the hills by themselves, are hoping to draw them into their fellowship before the bars with "Briars Welcome" signs do.

Richard Hudson of Cincinnati, director of church development for the Ohio Society of Christian Churches, told a workshop on mountain migrants:*

Certainly it seems to me established churches are going to have to look on the inner city as a primary mission alongside of foreign missions.

A lot depends on personal work. I doubt very much if any other group except the church is prepared to offer the entree for these people into metropolitan life. Religion is the natural background of these people, and it can serve as a natural entree.

We may have to divide the inner city into parish units small enough so individual pastors can pretty well know the neighborhood.

It might be wise to investigate the idea that church groups serve as sponsors for families as they come into the city, something along the lines of the displaced people program!

Meanwhile, Clete Allen shrugs his shoulders when asked about the big church on the corner. "Naw," he says, "they hain't interested in the likes of us."

---

* As quoted by Mary Ellen Wolfe in the Dayton *Journal Herald*, July 25, 1961.

HOPE IN THE ASPHALT JUNGLE

WE ARE IN THE URBAN AGE whether we like it or not. There is no going back to the good old days of grandma down on the farm. The inner city church is a prophecy of what is in store for the whole church in the urban age. If you are not in the inner city now, stay where you are, and you will be soon. We need to develop new strategies and new materials for what lies ahead.

As I write this we are preparing for the Vacation Bible School of this summer. We expect an enrollment of about two hundred. Over one hundred of these children will be Negro and Puerto Rican. They will come from public housing projects, from slum dwellings and from apartment houses. Many of them have never been out of the neighborhood, most of them have never lived in a suburban area. Perhaps half of them have never been out in the country. Life to them means being crowded into dirty run-down apartments. It means dodging trucks while playing ball among the garbage cans in the broken streets. It means having your lunch money taken away at the point of a knife almost every day.

Before me I have . . . Vacation Bible School publicity materials. The largest poster shows Christ (with a perma-

From an article by Erwin E. Prange, published in the *Walther League Messenger*, October, 1961.

SURE I LIVE ON THE STREETS, MAN. WHERE ELSE DO YOU GO WHEN THE FAMILY OR THE HEAT OR THE APARTMENT WALLS START CLOSING IN ON YOU?

I DON'T KNOW. I GUESS MY MISSION IS JUST TO GET THE MOST FUN OUT OF LIFE. IS THERE A BETTER ONE?

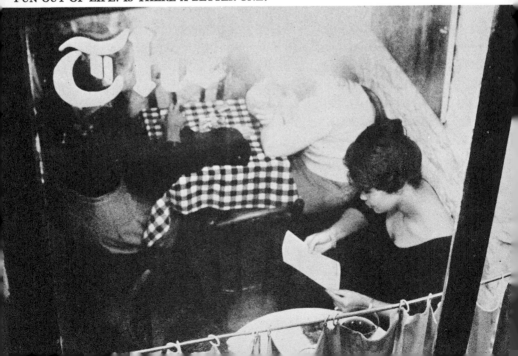

nent) holding a freshly laundered sheep. The setting is fantastically beautiful and looks even less like Palestine than Brooklyn. The post card shows three white children in beautifully starched clothing gaily skipping through a bower of trees toward a little country church. I sometimes wonder if religion is as unrealistic to children as these materials are. The whole thing is a kind of ecclesiastical bluebird land.

The tides of juvenile delinquency, crime and V.D. are rising on every side. Concerned people are "viewing with alarm" and wringing their hands in righteous frustration. Everyone is asking the same question, "What's wrong with our youth?" Very few seem to be searching their own hearts and asking, "What's wrong with the parents?", or "What's wrong with the society that we have all helped to create?" There is no shortage of scapegoats. Some blame it on permissive child training, others on overly strict parents. Some say it is the school, others accuse TV, the automobile and the Communists. We are terribly busy with crusades against dirty movies and magazines. Yet nothing seems to help. Are we perhaps trying to treat the symptoms rather than the disease itself?

What is wrong with our youth? What is wrong with our society? Some have suggested that we have lost our sense of mission. This is the age of the great goof-off, when plumbers don't plumb, repair men don't repair, salesmen don't sell, and, we might add, preachers often don't preach. You buy a new car and it looks as if it had been assembled by the inmates of a state institution. You buy a new suit in a fancy Fifth Avenue shop and the lining rips out in three weeks. If you study hard in school you are a grind, if you work hard on the job you are a scab, if you are honest you are a dope, and if you try to be decent you are a square. It's a frustrating age—no one seems to be really happy about it. Parents and children, employers and employees, producers and consumers seem to be equally frustrated.

How can we regain a sense of mission? The Church already has the greatest mission in the world—to proclaim Christ and Him crucified. Every believer has the tremendous mission to glorify God and enjoy Him forever.

How does this apply to youth? Youth is the time of mission. Contrary to popular mythology, teen-agers aren't just interested in playing games. They are looking for something real and something worthy of their tremendous vitality and imagination.

Some important steps in this direction have already been taken. . . . It has been suggested that we apply the Peace Corps plan to the problem of the inner city church. Full time youth volunteers could work during the summer and for full years in some of the run-down urban parishes. They would live in the area and be compensated for their expenses only. They would work with Vacation Bible Schools, Sunday Schools, and Youth Groups, make calls and conduct surveys.

Our inner city churches need dedicated manpower and womanpower even more than they need money. Our youth need a real mission. They need to know what life in the urban heartland of America is like. They need to know what the Church of the future will be. . . . It would be the bridge of communication and love between the now severed halves of the Body of Christ—the inner city and the rest of the church.

AN INSIDE VIEW . . .

CHICAGO JOURNAL

T HE MAXWELL STREET area of Chicago has always been one of the nation's roughest neighborhoods. Once Al Capone planned his battles with the real Elliott Ness from his headquarters there. Today, gangs roam the streets; family arguments may still be settled with knives, and sixty people may be crowded into a tenement building originally planned for two families.

It is Chicago's worst area for juvenile delinquency.

It was in this neighborhood ten years ago that a group of earnest young churchmen founded what they hoped would be a "worshiping and witnessing community"—the kind of church they felt Christ had in mind. They called it the West Side Christian Parish.

Today the Parish has three store front churches, a youth center, a counseling center, and an administrative office. But its real heart is not buildings but people—mostly young people.

There are usually about a dozen year-round volunteers and at least thirty summer volunteers on the staff of the Parish. Mostly of college age, they live in the Project House,

The items written by Dean Beery, Sue Crafton, Tom Reed, and Mac Eaton, have appeared in *Young People*, magazine of the American Baptist Publication Society.

81

a rickety converted tenement from which it took a month to shovel the debris when the parish bought it.

The volunteers live under the watchful eye of the Rev. Paul Crafton, a recent seminary graduate who has worked in the parish three years, and his pert young wife, Sue.

Making $10 a month (plus room, and board cooked by the volunteers but supervised by Sue, a home economics teacher), the young people of the staff may have to do anything from scrubbing floors to helping a drunken teen-ager home from a bar.

Three of the volunteers have been beaten; two have had cameras snatched out of their hands as they walked down the streets in broad daylight.

But, as Paul Crafton says, "missionary work is not a matter of shouting words, however true, to strangers at a distance." The volunteers live in the heart of the Maxwell Street area and do their best to make these brothers, now strangers, become friends.

How well they succeed—and sometimes fail—is shown on the following pages. These are diary items written by staff members as they worked with more than two hundred neighborhood youth, with some of the city's most vicious gangs, with broken families, and with earnest new Christians.

DEAR JOURNAL,

Tonight I was showing a movie in the Youth Center of the West Side Christian Parish when—"crash"! I caught the projector as it toppled from the bench. I looked up to see one of the teen-age boys heading for the door.

The movie, *Something of Value,* dealt with the relationship of two men, one white and one a Negro. They lived like brothers until the issue of personal convictions and obligations entered the picture, and the two men went in separate directions. At the climax of the movie they met face to face, and the white man killed the Negro.

The abrupt ending, along with his being a little drunk, made the movie too much for this Negro boy at the Youth Center. It had drawn out his deep feelings of resentment and prejudice until he kicked over the projector on his way out the door. As soon as I had set the projector up again I called after him, for I was hoping to find out the trouble and to show him that I was deeply concerned about him.

Four times I questioned him. The first three times I received the same answer, a fist in the chest. The fourth time, we passed on the street. He whirled around and came back to where I was, prepared to slug again. I stood with my arms at my sides, looking him in the eyes with a slight smile on my face. He stopped, looked at me, dropped his fists, and walked on down the street.

I don't think we are aware of the tremendous frustrations and mixed emotions that are pent up inside Negro teenagers here in this Parish as in many areas. To them it is a living hell to see white people continually strut their expensive clothes, for it contrasts their own limited opportunities and the fact that they always seem to get the dirty work. They burn inside, or take out their feelings on all of us.

Since I showed this boy that I was on his side no matter what he had done, that I wanted to help, and also that I wasn't afraid of him, we have been able to have some good conversations.

—TOM REED

DEAR JOURNAL,

I came to know what fear really means. I was handing a girl in my teen-age club some invitations to pass out when it happened.

I felt an arm around me and all of a sudden I saw stars and everything faded out.

When I awoke from the nightmare, I was being helped to my feet by an elderly man, as about thirty women, youth and children, some crying, looked on.

In broad daylight and in front of people who knew me I had been beaten up by a gang of fellows from the area in which we work.

For a great while afterwards I was afraid to walk alone on the streets. Though I had previously felt familiar with our neighborhood and had walked by myself from the Parish church to our house at night with few qualms, I suddenly realized that I had *many* qualms about doing so. The neighborhood did not seem familiar any more.

In thinking about the incident and several experiences that followed, I have come to a new understanding of the meaning of fear.

I noticed the same type of fear I was feeling in the people who live around our house. Adults and children who have little fear of moving around their own neighborhood view everybody with suspicion in a neighborhood several blocks away.

One of the ladies in our church said that she would never live in the suburbs because the people there are so "isolated" that it isn't safe; by the suburbanite's standards, however, the woman herself is living in one of the roughest sections of the country.

Children from the Parish who visited my home town, a quiet village in southern Ohio, as part of the Parish's "Friendly Town" program last summer, were surprised to see that we really didn't bar our front door.

As I reflect tonight on these things I have come to believe that much of our fear is irrational and it is fear based not on the known but on the unknown.

When a gang attacked me, I jumped to the instinctive conclusion that the whole community was a stranger and would attack me.

As I think about it, it seems almost necessary in relations between persons in our world that we have to know each other—before we can love each other.

—DEAN BEERY

DEAR JOURNAL,

One of the things I have been most impressed with in my work with the Parish has been the profound effect that segregation in housing has on people's lives. It has an effect not only on the minority group being discriminated against, but also on the majority group doing the discriminating.

I grew up in a small town in a homogeneous white neighborhood and although I was always taught that all men were created equal, it would have been very easy for me to form stereotypes of minority groups.

For example, if my only contact with Negroes had been in seeing them when driving through slum areas, it would be very easy for me to think that all Negroes live in slums and can't keep their property up.

After living and working in a Negro slum area for two

years, I begin to see that living in slums is not a racial characteristic. I see many very stable people and families who have the ability and money to get out. But the problem is where to go.

The great majority of homes in the Chicago area are not for sale to Negroes, and they are not sure what they will have to face from their neighbors in the ones that *are* for sale to them.

In Chicago the rent in the Maxwell Street area is higher per square foot than anywhere else in the city including the expensive "Gold Coast" apartments on the lake front.

On top of paying this fantastic rate of rent, they generally pay it to "absentee" landlords who take no responsibility for the property. There is big money in slum housing. I had a very interesting discussion with a teen-age club I have been working with on reasons for segregation in housing. Several of the young people thought it was "just because white people don't like us."

Segregation in housing with the accompanying feelings of resentment and inferiority on the part of the minority group and fear and superiority feelings in the oppressor is a vice we cannot afford to perpetuate in this country.

—DEAN BEERY

DEAR JOURNAL,

Tonight a group of teen-age fellows and I went to a Chinese restaurant for refreshments. We went because these fellows are interested in Chinese culture, and they wanted to see what a Chinese restaurant is like. The headwaiter showed us to a table which was in a separate room from

87

the rest of the restaurant. I wonder if this was because the fellows were Negro?

The waitress was a delight! You could tell she loved young people, and she had all the time and patience in the world despite her heavy work load. The fellows did not have much money and they were playing every angle and taking every factor into account before they ordered. They asked such questions as: "Do crackers come free with the soup?" It took them a half-hour to finally decide what they wanted. The waitress kept coming back to see if they were

ready, answering their foolish questions with good humor and kidding them a little.

When the fellows had ordered and eaten their food, they decided they wanted to tip the waitress because she had been such a good sport. I was amazed at these fellows; after they had haggled and schemed for half an hour to get as much food for as little money as they could (each order did not amount to over fifty cents), they pulled out quarters, dimes, and nickels. The tip finally amounted to almost as much as the bill! We could see that the waitress was sitting out in the other room eating her supper, but the fellows did not want to leave until she came back because they were afraid that old head waiter would get her tip. Finally, I persuaded them to leave, but as soon as they got out they went to the big picture window and waited there on the street for the waitress to come and pick up their tip. At last, I went back into the restaurant and told her about the tip. She was quite surprised that they had tipped her, she said, because she knew teen-agers did not have much money. I came back out as she went to our table to get the money, and outside the fellows were standing before the window with sheepish grins waving at her.

We walked down the street to the car and got in, but then, as we began to drive away, the waitress appeared at the door and motioned for me to come over to her. I got out of the car and walked over; I could see a tear in the corner of each eye. She just wanted me to thank the fellows, and tell them that she did not expect a tip.

I know they are fully capable of getting drunk, boarding a bus and scaring the bus driver out of his wits. In fact, I had not long ago helped to get them out of jail for that very thing. But tonight, I had seen another side. There was something about the incident that calls tears to my eyes when I think about it, for tonight I had seen people really open up and give of themselves.

—MAC EATON

DEAR JOURNAL,

The needs of the neighborhood daily press upon us. We never look from our windows without seeing the unkempt houses; we rarely walk up stairs to a house in the neighborhood without feeling them creak with rotting beneath us.

Again and again our high doorbell is rung by the outstretched finger of a child standing on tiptoe. I open the door, and a cute little Negro boy says, "C'n I come in? Just for ten minutes?"

But I turn away his plaintive request, though I realize that there is no father in his home, that his mother must work, that he does not receive the attention that a child needs for security. We do not feed and clothe the needy of our neighborhood.

How then, we are asked, can we call ourselves a Christian mission? If we turn children from our door and fail to feed and clothe, how can we claim to be spreading Christian love?

To attempt to feed and clothe the needy of Chicago's near West Side, to open Project House to every child who rings the doorbell (a physical impossibility considering the number of children in the overcrowded neighborhood) is to treat the *symptoms* and not the *causes* of man's suffering.

The Parish exists to proclaim the gospel. The gospel strikes at man's sin, the basic cause of child neglect and of the discrimination in housing which forces some Negroes to live in overcrowded, run-down sections.

What good does it do to feed and clothe, if those receiving gifts of food and clothing never learn to take responsibility for providing for themselves, and never learn to recognize the sin and selfishness of bringing children into the world without the stable family structure they need?

"Man shall not live by bread alone," and merely having certain physical needs met does not make a person fully human.

It is not just the sin of persons in the slums, or even the sins of persons in Chicago that we are faced with. We, the workers of the West Side Christian Parish, must face the evil we have done, the evil we have done as white persons in the days of slavery, when indiscriminate slave trading destroyed the Negro family structure.

We must face the evil we have done in segregating and in allowing segregation which forces people to live in slums, the evil done by the absentee landlord who refuses to repair his apartments because he knows that prejudice in housing assures him a profit from the rental of run-down slum apartments.

Greed in all of us goes to produce the suffering of the slums. It is the gospel which challenges a man to turn from his self-centeredness to an attitude of responsibility to his fellow man and to God.

So the Parish seeks to express the gospel in its store front church services, its youth fellowship meetings, its personal counseling, its Bible study meetings in members' homes, and in other activities.

But it does not try to deal just with manifestations of man's shortcomings. It seeks to get at the roots: sin and selfishness in the relationship of man to man and man to God.

—C. Tom Ross

Dear Journal,

As we become a part of the neighborhood here and go about our daily work, there are those few individuals we meet who bring real joy into life. Mrs. Williams is such a person.

Her six bright-eyed, healthy children often come into the Parish playlot eating big red apples, peaches, bananas, watermelon, and even hard-boiled eggs. As a home economics teacher, I appreciate the contrast between their diet and that of most of the other less healthy children who always have candy, potato chips, and soda pop in their hands.

Many times, Mrs. Williams and I have shared our ideas on the role of a mother in bringing up a family. I have gained more insights from her than she from me. Mrs. Williams has learned the extraordinary importance of knowing and treating each of her children as a living person—all six of them!

One evening last summer, the youth volunteers were having a party at Project House. Several children were playing on the front steps and continually ringing the doorbell to pester us.

The volunteer in charge of the party opened the door angrily and unthinkingly slapped the closest child.

The news spread through the neighborhood rapidly, and many mothers were threatening that if something like that happened to their child they would get revenge, very likely burn the house down.

But fortunately it was Mrs. Williams' child who had been slapped. In her helpful, understanding way, she came to discuss the incident with us and, as a result, helped us to understand the neighborhood better.

Negroes have prejudices against whites which can well be justified by American history. But between Mrs. Williams and myself there have come understanding and forgiveness through Christ, which enable us to face responsibly our common task of winning freedom and life abundant for ourselves and future generations.

* * *

The first Sunday I attended church at the West Side Christian Parish, I met an attractive young-looking lady. Much to my surprise, I found she was the mother of thirteen children!

Mrs. Brown always seems so calm and appears to be completely enjoying life.

One evening my husband and I visited in their home. Her husband and teen-age sons were gathered around the dining room table playing games. They spend many evenings together engaged in different activities. There was serious conversation, jokes, and periods of laughter. I had the feeling that I was participating in a real family.

Several times as my husband and I have taught different classes, the bright, beaming face of a Brown child has been there. It is such a pleasure to teach children who are eager to learn and try. Certainly the training and interest given them at home show through.

I am sure Mr. and Mrs. Brown have had real struggles in rearing their thirteen children. At times it would have been easier to let them spend evenings anywhere but home, or for them to have many outside activities which would get them out of the house. The time they have taken to become involved in the lives of the children is the most important thing they could have done.

—SUE CRAFTON

PANIC IN WESTWOOD

WHEN YOU DRIVE down the quiet, shady streets of West-wood, it doesn't look like a place that has been torn apart by panic.

But not many months ago, two out of every three homes in the community were for sale. People were leaving by the dozens; there were threatening phone calls at midnight, and police kept a close watch for the start of a riot at any moment.

All because the rumor was true: "The Negroes are moving into Westwood."

Westwood is a pleasant, quiet neighborhood of homes on the near west side of Dayton, Ohio—an industrial city of perhaps half a million people. In 1950, most of Westwood's 13,000 residents owned their homes—usually small, one-and-a-half story frame bungalows. Eighty-five per cent of the men worked in factories, making good money in such plants as National Cash Register, Frigidaire, or Delco.

In 1950, only 14 of Westwood's 4,165 homes had Negroes living in them.

In fact, the color line in Dayton had been kept as sharp as in a southern city up until World War II. Negroes rarely shopped downtown. They didn't use the "white" swimming pools nor eat in the better restaurants. They didn't sit any-where but in the balcony in the theaters.

The only place they could live was in the southwest quarter of the city—south of Third Street, the main east-west road through town, and west of Main Street, the north-south thoroughfare.

There they crowded into dilapidated homes, a whole family sometimes living in a single room. Most couldn't afford to buy a house; they were at the mercy of landlords who let the paint peel and the plaster fall while collecting fantastic rents. A family might not like to pay it, but they had no other place to go.

But Dayton's industry doubled overnight when war hit. Negroes by the thousands came north to fill the need for labor. Wright-Patterson Air Force base, the purchasing center for the whole Army Air Corps, hired hundreds of Negro clerks, accountants, and supervisors.

These new residents wrote back to the south about the relatively good life they found in Dayton. This brought more Negroes, mostly middle-class people from the cities, to Dayton.

Suddenly, the "prison" on the southwest side was no longer made up of people so poor they couldn't get out if they wanted to. Now it was overcrowded with people quite capable of improving their situation, if only there were a place to go.

The banks, loan companies, and real estate agents, who help determine in any city where Negroes can buy property, decided to "open" new sections. One of them was Westwood, located close to the "colored part of town."

That was when the "blockbusters" moved in. The first one (we're not sure who he was, because there were many) picked out a street on the south edge of Westwood and began knocking on doors.

"Hello," he said. "I'm a real estate agent, and I wondered if your house is also for sale today."

Then he watched carefully for the housewife's response. If she crisply informed him that the family had no plans to move, he would answer, "That's just wonderful. That's fine. I admire you folks for your attitude."

But if the lady seemed even faintly interested (perhaps because of the Negroes in rattletrap cars he had paid to drive slowly up and down the street several times during the week before) his line went something like this:

"Well, the colored folks are moving in fast, you know. And while I can see that you're not a prejudiced-type person, it's understandable that you want to live with your own kind. Now, let's talk about price."

As soon as the blockbuster had found a seller, he put up a huge red "FOR SALE" sign on the front lawn, where it could be seen from every other house in the block.

"Our block is going," wives would say when their husbands came home from work that evening.

"I hear so-and-so has a buyer already," one wife would say to another over the back fence.

"I'm sure you don't want to be the last one on the block," the real estate agent would say to the dubious ones. And he'd plant another sign.

The wave of selling flowed across Westwood from south to north. Young families, just getting settled, had to pick up and start over in another home; old couples who had planned to end their days in Westwood fled on a week's notice, much of their savings wiped out by the drop in prices.

Those white families that did not sell were constantly receiving polite, skeptical visits or phone calls from real estate men—often eight or ten such calls a week.

After a while the blockbusters didn't have to work any more. Panic, based on prejudice or on fear of falling house prices, did their work for them.

And the real estate agents counted their money.

One distributed a crudely-printed card which read:

BUY A HOME   EV 4-7893
REV. & MRS. R. L. JEFFERSON
YOUR REAL ESTATE AGENTS

The other side of the card read like this:

Marriage Counseling by Appointment
REV. R. L. JEFFERSON, EV 4-7893
The Praying Preacher, Pastor of
KING DAVID BAPTIST CHURCH

This "praying preacher," like his fellow blockbusters of both races, was making money two ways (not counting his preaching and marriage counseling).

For the first house on the block, he sometimes had to pay a higher-than-usual price. But for each house after that, the panicky owners accepted prices as much as $2,000 below normal—just to get out before the price went lower still.

The blockbuster would then turn around and sell the same house to a Negro engineer from the air base, eager to get out of the ghetto, for a price several thousand dollars higher than the going rate.

Some of the more unscrupulous dealers played rough, paying for repeated midnight phone calls, with a heavy, coarse voice with Negro accent asking for a wrong number.

But just as effective was the line used by Jefferson. "I think it's just wonderful that you're staying," he'd say. "We need to promote brotherhood and all. But I just hope you're not disappointed like so many others. . . ."

By 1960, Westwood was 60 per cent Negro with dozens of white families moving out every week.

Now that the panic is over, some sheepish ex-Westwooders are admitting how foolish the whole thing was.

"The Negroes didn't shove us out," says one man. "The whites just abandoned the place."

"With three thousand houses on the market in a year's time," says a realtor, "prices naturally went down. But if people had stayed calm and stayed put, their property wouldn't have been affected at all. These people played right into the hands of the blockbusters."

Those families that did stay get satisfaction out of telling their ex-neighbors the fact that houses in Westwood are now worth more—not less—than before the big panic!

The neighborhood, in fact, has really been spruced up.

Proud to have a home of their own in pleasant surroundings for the first time, many of the new residents keep their property neater than it ever was. The city planning board says new families have spent from $500 to $3000 each improving their homes in Westwood.

Residents, old and new, got together in a Neighborhood Council to prevent trends toward Westwood's ever becoming a slum. Community spirit has grown, helped along by hobby shows, flower shows, jazz concerts, and summer block parties.

But while things were settling down for many Westwood home owners, things were getting worse and worse for the churches.

There had been eight churches in the area, with not one Negro member among them. One by one during the panic, as offers came from Negro congregations to buy their buildings, seven of the churches looked at their shrinking membership lists—and sold out.

The chapter that follows is the story of the eighth church —the one church that dared to stay.

THE CHURCH THAT DARED TO STAY

"Pastor, either that nigger kid goes or I go. Which one is it going to be?"

The pastor looked at the people standing around in the hall, trying to act as though they hadn't heard.

Then he looked at Phil, a teen-ager whose large size and black skin made him stick out like an exclamation point in the junior high department. Phil sat stiffly in his chair, staring straight ahead.

"I'll say it once more," shouted Mr. Kaytes. "Either he goes or I go. What have you got to say about that?"

"Well," said Bob. . . .

But we're getting ahead of our story.

Westwood Church had just moved into a beautiful, modern building which filled a complete city block in the heart of the community. But what seemed far more important, as the church council looked at its dwindling membership, was that there was still a $75,000 debt on the building.

How many more members would move away? Could the church last long enough to pay off the debt?

A determined, idealistic group of council members felt that the only hope for the church was to try to serve the neighborhood, no matter who lived there. At a poorly attended council meeting they passed a resolution stating that any person, regardless of race, would be welcome as a member of Westwood Lutheran Church.

103

Report of the action spread swiftly from home to home in the parish. The next council meeting had 100 per cent attendance, and after a heated argument the action of the previous meeting was reversed!

Stunned, outraged, the pastor resigned.

It wasn't long afterward that the church approached Bob Secrist, then pastor of a church in Cleveland. The Westwood pulpit committee had heard that he was successfully leading a congregation made up of Italians, Negroes, poor whites, university students, and wealthy socialites.

"We came to Dayton to meet with the council," Bob remembers. "We stood on the sidewalk and looked down the street. On every average block of nine houses, three had been sold and three had "FOR SALE" signs in front.

"And we'd been told that two of the remaining three would consider any reasonable offer."

Before the meeting with the council, Secrist talked with real estate men, city officials, Community Chest workers and anybody else who could tell him about Westwood. He walked the streets, engaging in conversation anybody who would talk about the area.

That night, the councilmen started off with small talk. But eventually they came to the point:

"Pastor Secrist, what do you think should be done about the colored people?"

He was ready. "I don't think it's right to seek people out and urge them to come just because their skin is black."

Several councilmen breathed a sigh of relief.

"But," he went on, "I believe this church is here to spread the gospel, and I think it should try to reach all who need Christ. Colored or white."

There was a long silence before discussion started again. But when it came time to vote, even most of those who had helped to reverse the "anybody welcome" motion months before voted to call Secrist as pastor.

"Some of the leaders of the council," Bob believes, "felt they could control the pastor no matter what he said. So they didn't object."

But the council ran up against determination immediately when Bob, with his red-headed vivacious wife, Joan, and three children moved to Dayton.

The council offered to sell the parsonage in Westwood and find one in a "nicer" part of town, where the school wasn't mostly colored.

"Not on your life," said the new pastor. "I want to live in the community I serve. Besides, who will want to join my church if he knows I want him as a member but not as a neighbor?"

His blunt, realistic approach showed up, too, at the very first meeting he and Jo attended. "It was the Home Builders Class," he recalls, "and it was aptly named. Every couple there was building a home somewhere outside of Westwood!"

The new pastor interested the class in helping with a frank, objective study of the congregation, the community, and their future. They accepted the idea.

Months later, when all the facts had been tabulated, Bob decided to present the results of the study as his annual report. A national urban church expert who had been helping him advised against doing this. "There's not a hopeful sign in it," he said.

Bob agreed that things looked grim. "I was writing letters

of transfer right and left. Our membership was down from over a thousand to around six hundred. You could see the congregation would be a goner in two years if some definite changes were not made.

"I decided the best thing to do would be to scare the heck out of them."

Here are some of the phrases from the printed report:

"Our communing membership is down from 701 at the end of last year to 626 at the end of 1959. This is more than a 10 per cent loss. . . . Where do these figures carry us if we think ahead?"

"We are in the black today only because we did not pay our benevolences, but diverted that money to current expenses."

"In 1954 you had 551 members of Westwood Church living within one mile of the church. Today you have less than half that many, 209. Think ahead."

"There seems to be a tendency to want to avoid the subject of the future of Westwood Lutheran Church. . . . No church has any cause for existence except that its people are fulfilling Christ's command to be his witnesses! Are we?"

A series of charts and graphs followed, showing such items as the fact that Sunday church school offerings had dropped 45 per cent in three years and that attendance was half what it had been in 1957.

The congregation listened and then accepted Bob's suggestion that a large committee be set up, to evaluate the study and recommend which of three choices the congregation should take: move to another location, stay and try to serve, or disband.

The president of the congregation made an enthusiastic

speech praising the idea—and soon afterward asked for his letter of transfer!

But there were many who had supported the new pastor all along and continued to do so—some because they firmly believed in the brotherhood of man, and many because they believed this was the right thing to do even though they had to overcome life-long prejudices.

At an early meeting, a sociologist from nearby Hamma Divinity School told them frankly what happens to churches that stay in racially-changing neighborhoods.

"There's a sudden drop at first," he said, pointing to a graph. "Then there's always this leveling-out, which is where your church is right now. Your attendance is half what it was two years ago.

"From there, a church can either go up or down, depending on how successfully they reach the new residents of the community."

When he had finished, committee members began firing questions.

"If we open the doors to Negroes, won't they come flooding in and take over the church?"

"No. Experience shows that if you work extra hard, you may be able to interest twenty Negroes in attending here by the end of a year. It'll take you another year to get twenty more. "The color of a man's skin doesn't make him any easier to reach with the gospel than anybody else."

"What about finances? Don't they give a lot less?"

"In the first place, your finances can't get worse than they are. But you'll find that colored members—just like white members—will give liberally when they are trained in stewardship and understand the program of the church."

107

A CHURCH THAT DARES TO STAY IN A CHANGING NEIGHBORHOOD MUST BE READY

TO FACE PROBLEMS AND, IN A SPIRIT OF LOVE, WORK OUT THE ANSWERS.

"Will they help with the leadership, or just sit in the pew?"

"Just like any other human being, the Negro member will pitch in and help if he feels his help is wanted and respected."

"Won't the majority of the white people quit the congregation when the Negroes start coming?"

"There are always a few who quit, but far fewer than you'd expect. The people who are deeply prejudiced make a lot of noise, but when they quiet down or leave, most of the people will still be here. Even most of those with prejudices dinned into them since childhood will stay because they feel it's the right thing to do. You'll still have losses, of course, because of moving."

There were two more such meetings in the following months, with more of the same kind of discussion. As old fears were aired, many of them faded away.

The new pastor, meanwhile, was calling on board members and attending all organizational meetings—and steering the conversation around to the future of the church at every opportunity. He also was talking with Urban League executives, the Area Council people, P.T.A. and school officials, and even the police. He was getting to know his community better than some people who had lived there all their lives.

Members of the congregation were doing something just as important, though. In groups of five or six, they began meeting in homes for a series of weekly Bible studies. The material furnished them by the pastor was based on 1 Corinthians—Paul's letter to people in trouble in an urban church.

"No, it was not a coincidence," Secrist admits with a grin. "We had to discuss Christ's will for us in our particular situation if we followed the Bible passage at all."

Meanwhile, though, Westwood Church remained almost "lily-white." True, a few Negro children attended the Vacation Bible School, one was in catechism class, and two little girls came to Sunday school. But the majority of the adults in the church never saw them.

Teen-agers in catechism class were rough on Phil, the Negro boy who had started to attend. "Big black ape," and "coon," they called him.

Pastor Secrist, though, blames pressure from parents for the teen-agers' actions. "You're going back to that class with a black boy in it?" some parents would ask every Saturday.

Eventually Phil quit, despite the pastor's attempts to make him feel welcome. But he did agree to come to Sunday school occasionally.

And that's where Mr. Kaytes found him, on the morning we were telling about when we started this chapter.

Bob got out of his borrowed black Ford (a sideswipe accident the day before had taken the doors off his own) and walked into the assembly hall.

Mr. Kaytes was steaming. "Well, Pastor, I see you got a black one."

"Well, it's not mine, it's just borrowed. . . ."

"No," Kaytes said loudly, "I mean that nigger over there." People stopped in their tracks.

"If he stays, I go," Mr. Kaytes declared.

"Can you say that as a Christian?" the pastor asked.

"Never mind. If he stays, I go." His voice kept rising. "What are you going to do, Pastor? It's him or me."

"In that case, Mr. Kaytes,"—Bob stuck out his hand—"I'm sorry, and good-by."

Things were popping in the council too. The church was facing more serious money worries; how long could they hold out? There were feelers from several Negro churches about buying the property; should they sell while they could?

Members were still moving out of the area. And while the city's other Lutheran pastors had praised Westwood's work, they were only too glad to accept the letters of transfer of those who came into their area. Bob Secrist knows of only one pastor who encouraged a Westwood member to stay with the congregation.

And as if that weren't enough, the motion to welcome people of all races—the motion that had led to a council fight in the first place—was introduced again in a council meeting!

By now the congregation had a president, an alert young engineer named Carl Deis, who was very much in favor of staying and serving the neighborhood. The council, however, was still divided on the question.

Carl let debate over the motion run on for a long, hot evening. Pent-up feelings were let loose; people had a chance to say what they really thought.

Then, just as they were ready to vote on the motion, Carl got them to table it. The "anti-Negro" group relaxed, surprised but relieved.

"Whose side are you on, anyway?" a friend asked him later. "We could have passed it, this was our chance." Carl just smiled.

Before the next council meeting, several other Negro

children had wandered into the Sunday school and, finding no repeat of the Kaytes incident, had come again.

At council the motion was debated vehemently again. Once again it was tabled.

And a third time the council met, arguing hotly the same motion—until suddenly Carl ruled that the whole discussion was out of order!

"The motion is illegal," he said. "Always has been. The constitution of any United Lutheran congregation lists only one requirement for membership: that a person accept Jesus Christ as Lord and Savior.

"We as a council have no right to set up any other requirements—and neither does anyone else!"

They saw the point. And the hours of talking out their fears had helped some of the "antis" become at least resigned to the idea of an integrated fellowship.

One such council member who had been most vocal now had two Negro boys in his junior church school class, and was making them feel welcome! Darker faces were becoming a common sight in many classrooms.

And an active evangelism committee was being formed of people willing to knock on every door for thirty blocks around, seeking unchurched people and inviting them to church.

There were still tense moments. One night a shy, quiet Negro girl slipped in a side door and came to Pastor Secrist's study while the Luther League members were busily preparing for a big youth rally. Laura had been in Sunday school and in catechism, but she knew there never had been a Negro youth at Luther League. Would she be welcome?

Bob looked out into the hall. He saw two girls, both of

whom he'd heard make strong, prejudiced statements, setting up the registration table.

"I just took her right over there," he says with a grin, "and asked those two girls to show her how to help register the delegates as they arrived."

"The next time I saw them the three were in the kitchen, wiping dishes. And the next time I saw them, they were sitting together in Sunday school.

"From then on, Laura came to Luther League meetings."

Bob admits that the first few sessions "seemed a little strained." The kids wanted to make her welcome, but nobody knew what to do. "They treated her as if she were made of glass."

It's different today. "You can go to a Luther League picnic," Bob says, "and if a guy can't get the ball over the plate, he gets razzed—whether he's white or colored. The stiffness is gone."

The same is becoming true of the adult activities of the church today. Westwood Church has about 60 Negro members (out of about 550) as this is being written.

For the first time since 1958, the church's statistics show a net gain in membership. Church attendance is up by an average of forty persons a Sunday over the year before. And giving, as the sociologist had predicted, is increasing steadily.

The big problem is leadership. White families continue to move out of the neighborhood (usually for normal reasons: the panic is long over and houses are now worth *more* than they were before the blockbusters went to work!). Society, which has usually given a secondary role to the Negro and made it almost impossible for him to get a job

114

with much responsibility, just hasn't trained most of the Negro members for leadership roles. And most of Westwood's new members have never been active in a church before.

This the Westwood congregation hopes to work out with the help of an extra person on the church staff who will train the newer members for leadership.

Meanwhile, the new members are active in every area of the church's life—teaching Sunday school and Bible school; serving on the evangelism committee, the altar guild, and the census teams; keeping records and working on every committee of the church (*not*, the pastor emphasizes, because they're Negroes, but because they are members and are interested).

Phil, whose appearance in Sunday school set Mr. Kaytes raving, is an active Luther Leaguer and an acolyte in morning worship. Mr. Kaytes has never come back.

And the boy who had been most cruel to Phil in catechism class—who made Phil drop out of catechism for a year—is back in the church. He's a 17-year-old Sunday school teacher, with several very welcome Negro youngsters in his class.

Some other problems have cropped up.

One is that all of the other seven churches in the area have now been sold to Negro congregations. This means that it is harder to find families who are not being served by a nearby church.

It means, too, that the Westwood Lutheran congregation doesn't feel quite the sense of mission it did when it was the only church in Westwood willing to minister to Negroes.

"There was a tension and a goal as this congregation

moved toward integration of the races," Bob wrote recently to a denominational official.

"Now that integration (at least in its outward appearances) is an accomplished fact, there seems to be a feeling of 'Well, we did it! Now what do we do with it?'"

Another problem, about which Bob is hesitant to speak but which is very real, is the lack of co-operation—and in some cases active opposition—of the Negro ministers of the city.

Time and time again, families that were not active in their own churches have started coming to Westwood Lutheran—only to drop out because of insistent pressure from their "own" pastor.

"This is not a racial thing," says one white minister who knows the situation. "It's the normal jealousy of an unthinking minister who doesn't want to lose a name off his rolls, even of an inactive person.

"But Negro pastors who have made bold pronouncements about equality in the pew must have a little more vision, a little more action, than they have shown so far."

Nobody knows what the church will be like five years from now. Perhaps its problems are just starting. But the members are determined that the church will still be there, and that it will be seeking to serve Westwood in the way Christ wants it to.

AS PEOPLE OF DIFFERENT CULTURES WORK
TOGETHER THEY DISCOVER THAT
UNDERNEATH THEIR VARIED EXTERIORS
LIES THE COMMON STUFF
OF HUMANITY.

MY BROTHER
IS A STRANGER

WHETHER WE LIVE IN THE CITY
OR JUST VISIT IT SOMETIMES,
EVERY PERSON IN THE CROWD AND
TRAFFIC IS OUR BROTHER AND
EVERY BROTHER—FINALLY—
IS A STRANGER.

MANY A STRANGER-BROTHER THROWS
UP A PROTECTIVE WALL. HE DOESN'T
WANT MY FRIENDSHIP. OR IS SOME
OF THE SUSPICION ON MY PART

IN THE CITY WHO CARES ENOUGH ABOUT THE PERSON NEXT TO HIM TO START

CONVERSATION; WHO BREAKS DOWN THE BARRIERS OF INDIFFERENCE?

SIGNS, BY STRANGERS, DECLARE THE EMPTINESS WHERE PEOPLE USED TO LIVE . .

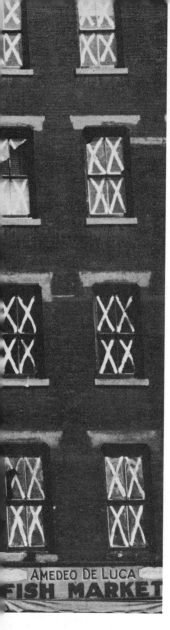

SOME SIGNS SHOUT, "STAY OUT!"

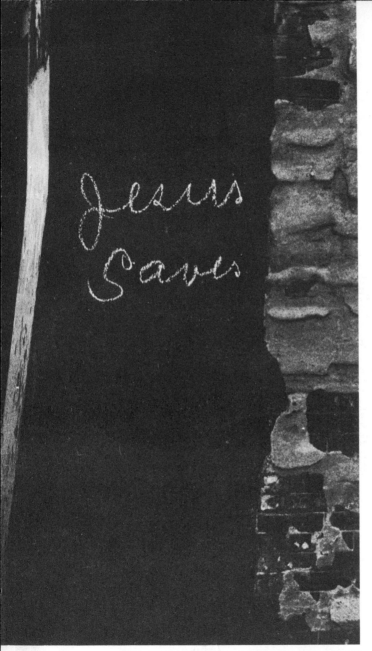

AND THE HIGHEST TRUTH MEN KNOW
LOSES ITS MEANING WHEN SCRAWLED ON
WALLS BY PEOPLE YOU NEVER SEE . . .

ALL AROUND ARE PEOPLE; SIGNS OF LIFE ARE EVIDENT.
BUT HOW CAN AN OUTSIDER GET THROUGH TO THEM?

YET SOME, THEIR CHILDISH HEARTS STILL PURE,
HARDLY KNOW THE WALLS ARE THERE . . .

... OTHERS, WHO HAVE COME UP HARD AGAINST THE WALL, ARE
WILLING TO FIND A WAY THROUGH; TO TURN STRANGERS INTO
FRIENDS AND BROTHERS. WILL YOU MEET THEM HALFWAY?

Photographs, except those noted below,
are by Edward Wallowitch.

Christian Photographers: 8-9, 12 (left), 32-33, 41, 44, 76.
 Ford Foundation: 65, 70, 71.
 New York *Daily News*: 12 (right), 13.
 Charles Harbutt: 38-39.

3253